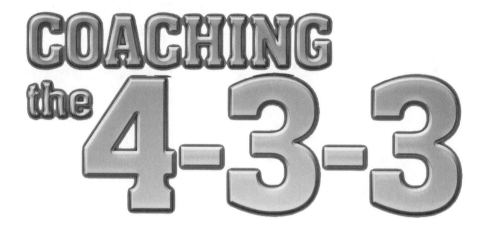

COACHING the 4-3-3

by Massimo Lucchesi

REEDSWAIN PUBLISHING

**Library of Congress
Cataloging - in - Publication Data**

by Massimo Lucchesi
    Coaching the 4-3-3

ISBN No. 1-59164-099-7
Lib. of Congress Catalog No. 2005926723
© 2005

Translation from Italian
Sinclair de Courcy Williams

*Cover Design, Layout and
Proofing*
Bryan R. Beaver

Printed by
DATA REPRODUCTIONS
Auburn, Michigan

Reedswain Publishing
562 Ridge Road
Spring City, PA 19475
800.331.5191
www.reedswain.com
info@reedswain.com

AUTHOR'S FOREWORD

The 4-3-3 is one of my favorite playing systems. Though I am inclined to think that no single playing system is intrinsically better than any other and that when it comes down to it the interpretation of the players is more important than the actual system in use, I particularly like the 4-3-3 because of the variety of attacking solutions that it can provide.

Another thing I very much appreciate about the 4-3-3 is its great flexibility in the defense phase. To give an example, the way you defend will be determined by how far back the wings are moving, and in this way the back's diagonal onto the weak side can be given more or less accentuation as the case may be.

In the book I will be trying to highlight the steps which I consider essential if you wish to give tactical organization to a team, particularly one using the 4-4-3.

My guiding aim is to estimate and bring out the tactical principles that will give adequate team organization and allow the players to follow the exercises so that the group can acquire the principles in question and make them their own.

It goes without saying that what I am giving here is only a practical proposal which the coach does not have to take up in all its parts. He will be able to integrate and expand it by following his own experience and his own ideas, making the right assessments of the situation in which he is working.

Massimo Lucchesi

STEP 1

ASSESSING THE PLAYERS' CHARACTERISTICS

Just as you need good musicians if you are going to play good music, so a coach needs good players to give his team effective play.

One thing should be said, however - it is never right to make unqualified judgments about players. No matter how talented a player appears to be, he will have his strong points and his 'doubtful' side.

The coach's job is to have a complete overview of his athletes' characteristics and, on that basis, to set down the most appropriate developments that can be made to the proposed playing system. Neither do I believe that any team can express itself better using one system instead of another.

The fundamental thing in my opinion is not the actual playing system used by the team, but rather how it is interpreted.
Quite apart from the playing system that has been selected, choosing the best flow of play and the right interpretation of the non-possession phase in connection with the natural talents of the players - these are the things that will bring up the levels of the team's performance.

THE 4-3-3 SYSTEM: STRONG AND WEAK POINTS.

Like every other playing system, the 4-3-3 has its strong and its weak points.

For the most part, these are not all-purpose truths, however, but specific problems than can come up in relation to the tactical face-off with the opposition's system.

We will now have a look at some of the typical characteristics of the 4-3-3.

Coaching the 4-3-3

In the non-possession phase the 4-man defense line seems capable of giving adequate coverage along the whole width of the playing field.

And yet that might not be quite true, in particular when the team is defending from low down, and the backs are placed on a level with their penalty area.

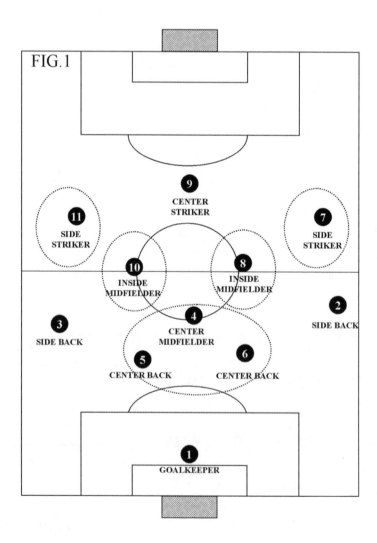

FIG.1

In this type of context, in particular if the team does not have wings capable of moving far downfield, the opponents will often find space on the weak side of the defense section.

The presence of the three center mid-fielders, two inside and one in the middle, guarantees solidity in the center of the field and, thanks to the work carried out by the center mid-fielder who acts as a filter, reduces the opposing strikers' opportunities of receiving the ball at their feet.

The placement of the three strikers favors offensive pressing, especially when the team forces the opposing defense section to move the ball to their side defenders, so creating the opportunity to shorten in towards the strong side (i.e., where the ball is being played).

Generally speaking, players who go on the field using the 4-3-3 are naturally inclined to press their opponents when the ball is being played in the areas highlighted in Figure 1:

* In the side zone on a level with the opposing defense section;
* In the central zone on a level with the mid field section;
* In the central zone in front of their own defense section.

On the other hand it is difficult with the 4-3-3 to close off a player in possession placed:

* In the central zone of your own defense section;
* Half way between the side defender and a wing in the classic position of inside mid-fielder;
* In depth, in the side zone 'above' the side back.

THE MAIN CHARACTERISTICS OF THE PLAYERS INTERPRETING THE 4-3-3.

Center defenders: these must be particularly good at dealing with the field behind them. The presence of the center mid-fielder who acts as a sort of screen helps them to handle their movements against the striker.

Side defenders: speed is one of their most important qualities, as well as being able to sum up the tactical situation on the field quickly and efficiently. The fact that the wing is not moving back (he would go to occupy the weak side acting as a 5th man) very often forces the side defender to lengthen out the defense diagonal so that the flanks will not be left too wide open.

Center mid-fielder: playing in front of the defense, he must be good at filtering, working as a screen and setting attacking plays in motion by acting as a downfield playmaker.

Inside mid-fielders: having to cover a fairly large area of the field, these two players need to be dynamic. They have important tasks to perform both in the possession and the non-possession phase, and these must be carried out with diligence, perseverance and efficiency.

Side striker: if you want to use effective attacking plays the importance of the wings' characteristics cannot be underlined enough. The side striker must be able to create the basis for finishing touches by his ability to receive in space, to dribble round his direct opponent, his knack at filtering in the ball and crossing tightly from the end line.

Center striker: as he is the only point of reference in the middle, the center forward must be very good at playing the dump and rebound, helping the team to gain field and acting as the attacking terminal when his team mates are using finishing touches.

THE TRIANGLE AND THE CHAINS OF THE 4-4-3.

The placement on the field of the players in a team using the 4-3-3 allows us to come up with a great number of playing triangles and 'chains'.

'Chains' are small groups of players (usually 3 or 4) placed close together and ready to develop certain attacking combinations.

The typical chains of the 4-3-3 are made up of:

* Side defender - inside mid-fielder - wing (side chain)
* Wing - center forward - wing (in depth chain)
* Inside mid-fielder - wing - center forward

By using the linked-in movements of the subgroups set out above, it will be possible for the coach to mark out certain attacking themes which will develop using coordinated movements.

STEP 2

BUILDING UP

THEORY

When you have the characteristics of every single player in the team clear in your mind, the next thing is to have a careful look at the possible developments of the playing system.

The team needs to be perfectly organized both in the phase of possession and non-possession, and it must also be well able to interpret the transitions (going from the attacking to the defense phase and vice versa).

It may be a personal thing, but my analysis starts from the attacking phase, though in some cases it could be better to begin teaching your players defense, particularly when those you have on hand do not know the 4-3-3 and do not give you enough security in the non-possession phase.

Once they have regained possession and consolidated that by an efficient administration of the post-conquest phase, the first aim that my team will be going for in the attacking phase is to get near to the opponents' goal so as to create the basis for finishing touch play.

In four words: sharpen build-play.

If it is true, as I believe, that sharpening build-up play results in creating the basis for finishing touches, then it is of fundamental importance that the team manages:

1. to bring the ball to parts of the field from which it will be possible to create effective scoring chances;
2. to create a situation which gives the player in possession enough time and space to initiate the scoring chance once he has arrived to such a part of the field.

Coaching the 4-3-3

In a nutshell, and to be as simple and as clear as possible, in the build-up phase the team tries to get past the opponents' midfield in order to give one of its members the chance to carry out finishing touches near the opponents' defense section.

From a practical point of view, the build-up phase can be interpreted in one of three ways: vertical, mixed or horizontal.

In the first case, the team will make principal use of long passes in developing its move into depth.

In the second case (mixed maneuvers) the team will be looking for more complex operations made up of a vertical pass followed by a dump involving the players in the vertical chains.
Last of all, if the team is building up horizontally the players will be principally making the ball roll around the inside of one section.

In consideration of the variety of possible developments in the build-up phase, and with the double aim of making your own plays into depth as confusing as possible while at the same time tightening up your countermoves against the opponents' tactics for facing them, each of our players needs to be able to choose the best solution from four options open to him:

• dump (or opening up) pass
• diagonal pass
• vertical pass
• long pass

The dump pass is useful because it gives the team different playing possibilities when the member in possession can no longer develop play in such a way as to gain depth.

The diagonal pass is fundamental to good horizontal build-up, giving the player entering into possession the chance to at least move the ball ahead.

The vertical pass can be used for the mixed development of building up play, while the long pass will allow us to get to the strikers at once, over the heads of any opposition in the opposing mid field.

It goes without saying that each of these ways of building up has its pros and cons. It is the coach's job to indicate the best flow of play, keeping in mind the tactical context in which the team is working and the match-ups against the contenders on the field (e.g., if we normally make good use of long passes in the build-up phase so as to take advantage of our center striker's ability in the air, it might be a good idea to modify our play in cases where he is not able to prevail in this way against the defender who is marking him).

ON THE FIELD

To upgrade the build-up phase and make it more efficient, we can work on schematic plays or situations.

If we want to use schematic plays the important thing is:
- that the player in possession has playing options;
- that the player without the ball (the receiver) has been supplied with the right signals and passing lines.

The coach defines the signals when he indicates the possible receivers in relation to the player in possession.

By defining playing options, signals and passing lines you determine the team's axis of play.

If you prefer to develop situational build-up, it is a good idea to set down the principles (universal rules).

SITUATIONAL BUILD-UP PHASE

As I have said before, the main aim of the build-up phase is to bring the ball forward, moving it up from an area towards the back (e.g., the 5th line) to somewhere more in depth while at the same time getting past the opposing mid-field section.

To get a better grasp of the idea, it might be useful to mark out the placement lines on which the team forms ranks when they are in the phase of non possession.

The following figure shows the placement on the 5 lines of the 4-3-3 system.

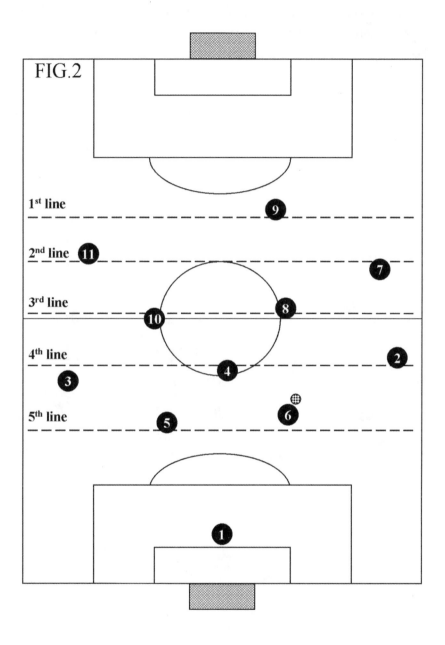

FIG.2

1st line

2nd line

3rd line

4th line

5th line

Coaching the 4-3-3

In order to identify the different lines on which the team is fielded we can highlight the various sectors (or parts of the field) as shown in the following figure.

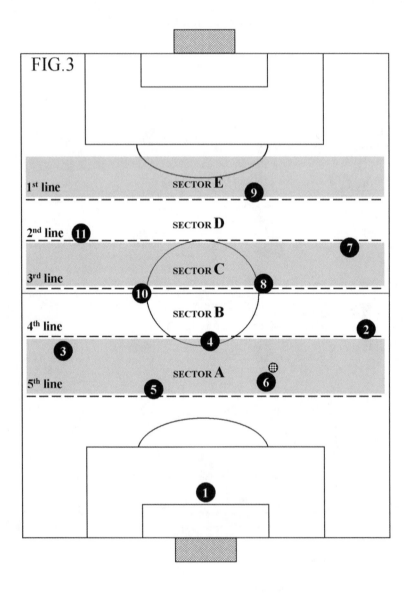

The intent is to get the ball from sector A to sector D by using the following principles (rules):

1. to move the ball to a sector immediately above (next to the one from which the ball starts off, e.g., from sector A to sector B or from B to C) you must use diagonal passes. This is because a diagonal pass will enable whoever is receiving it to play the ball forward.
2. to move the ball to a sector that is not immediately above (e.g., from sector A to C or from B to D) the best thing is to use a pass that is not exactly vertical to be followed by a dump.
3. whenever it is not possible to carry out a diagonal pass to bring the ball into the adjacent sector, it is best that the player who has carried out the pass follow it up so as to give support to the team mate who has just received.

Using the principles set out above will automatically create rules of conduct both for the player in possession and the one without the ball.

In practice this means that with the right center defender (n. 6) in possession, the right side defender (n. 2) and the center mid fielder (n. 4) will take up position in such a way as to be able to receive a diagonal pass, while the players placed in sectors that are more in depth (n. 7, 8 and 9) will get ready to receive a vertical pass.

In cases where 6 goes for a pass to 7 as in the diagram, 2 and 4 will then get in place (during the movement of the ball) to give support to and act as dumps for the player who receives.

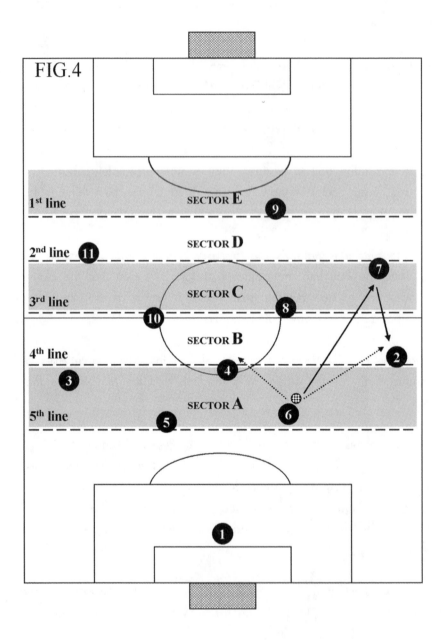

FIG.4

When n. 7 dumps on 2, n. 8 places himself to receive the diagonal pass while n. 9 gets into position to take delivery of the vertical pass.

If n. 2 plays on 9, n. 7 and 8 will give support, ready to receive the dump.

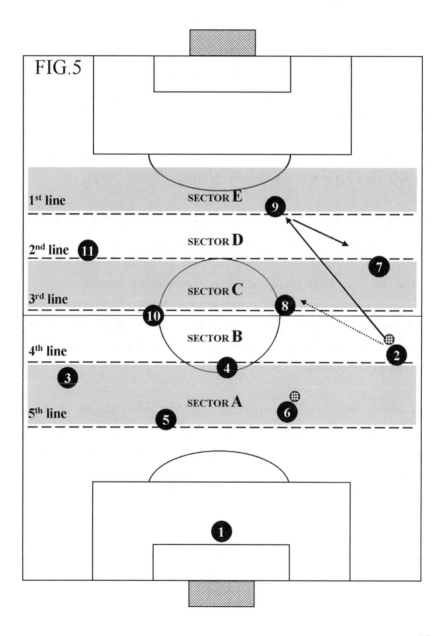

FIG.5

The very frequent flows of play as set out in figures 4 and 5 are simple examples of how the ball can be moved (and so go forward) from sector A to D following the situational principles we have set out.

SCHEMATIC BUILD-UP PHASE

As we have already seen, building up in a schematic way means finding solutions for the player in possession, which will call for the participation of the player without the ball, who must at the same time break free of marking.

The connection between playing solutions and getting free of marking will determine the team's axis of play.

Apart from being useful in the build-up phase, identifying the axis of play is important when you are laying down plans for finishing touches. Once you have defined the axis of play, it will in fact be simpler to find ways to link it up to the finishing touches.

With the 4-3-3 system, it is possible to define a good number of alignments of play, singling out the different roles of the players in the chains in question.

This variety will certainly make the attacking developments of the 4-3-3 more unpredictable and more difficult to defend. At the same time, however, it will also create problems in terms of general organization in cases where the team's reflexes are not clear or well put together.

Very often, the task of the single member of a chain will change in relation to the axis of play in use and this can create confusion and inevitable standstills in playing procedures.

What you need to have is a possible diagonal outlet, a vertical outlet (accompanied by a movement in support) and a long outlet (also accompanied by a movement in support) and so it becomes necessary to make the players' movements and their tasks as clear and as compatible as possible.

It stands to reason that the players supporting the strikers on long passes will not be able at the same time to go to meet the defenders in order to receive the ball at their feet.

AXIS OF PLAY

I will be setting out a number of typical flows of play applicable to the 4-3-3. These are not in relation one to the other.

Center defender in possession.

The center defender will normally have the following options:

1. a play towards the side: diagonal outlet on the side defender;
2. a play towards the inside: diagonal pass towards the center mid fielder;
3. a vertical play: pass in direction of the inside mid fielder or towards the wing coming up to meet it;
4. a long pass: in the direction of the center forward.

In Fig. 6 and 7 we illustrate the playing options open to the right center defender.

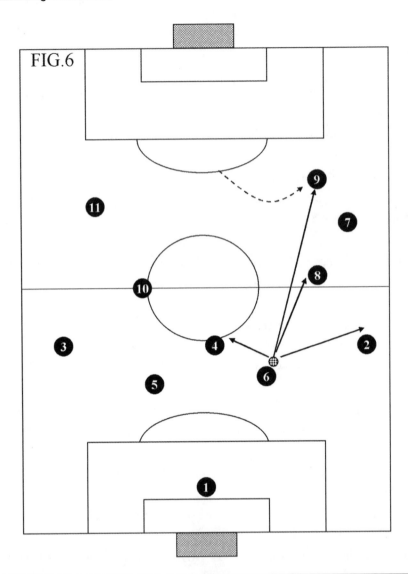

FIG.6

Dumping option (outlet)	**SIDE DEFENDER**
Diagonal option	**CENTER MID FIELDER**
Vertical option	**INSIDE MID FIELDER**
Long pass	**CENTER FORWARD (with WING in support)**

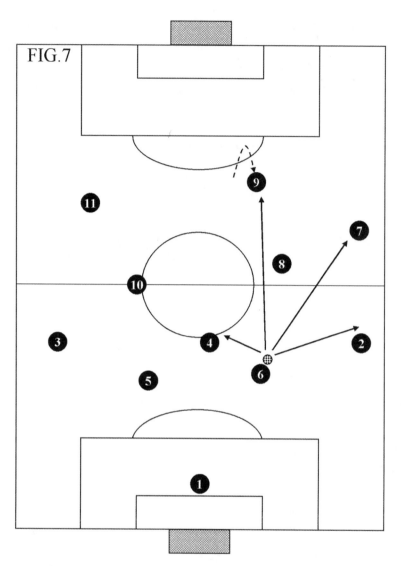

FIG.7

Dumping option (outlet)	**SIDE DEFENDER**
Diagonal option	**CENTER MID FIELDER**
Vertical option	**WING**
Long pass	**CENTER FORWARD (with INSIDE MID FIELDER in support)**

The main reason why it is important to define the flow of play is to make sure, for example, that the wing and the inside mid fielder do not both move towards the ball, leaving the center forward without the necessary support in cases where he is to receive a long pass.

SIDE DEFENDER IN POSSESSION

The following are the typical options open to the side defender:

1. dump on the nearby center defender;
2. a play towards the inside: diagonal pass for the center mid fielder;
3. a vertical play: pass for the wing or the inside mid fielder who comes to meet it;
4. long pass: for the center forward who frees himself of marking by coming forward or by deviating the ball onto the flanks.

When there are good margins of safety, the side back should follow the vertical movement of the ball when he has sent it in the direction of a player (inside mid fielder or wing) immediately in front of him.

This will not only make the team more dynamic and create more problems for the opponents' defense, it will also give the player in possession a greater number of solutions to choose from.

Figures 8 and 9 show the various possible solutions to be used by the right side defender.

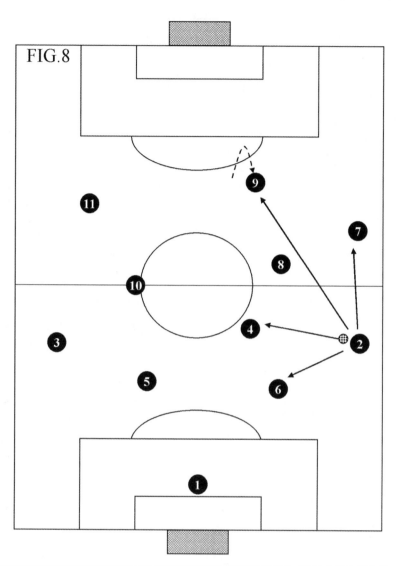

FIG.8

Dumping option (outlet)	**CENTER DEFENDER (KEEPER)**
Diagonal option	**CENTER MID FIELDER**
Vertical option	**WING (with CENTER MID FIELDER in support)**
Long pass	**CENTER FORWARD (with INSIDE MID FIELDER in support)**

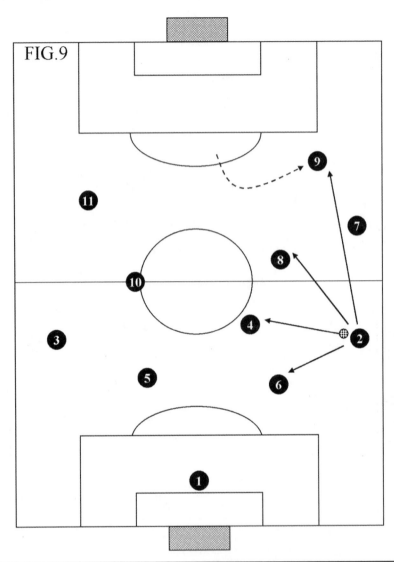

FIG.9

Dumping option (outlet)	**SIDE DEFENDER**
Diagonal option	**CENTER MID FIELDER**
Vertical option	**INSIDE MID FIELDER (with CENTER MID FIELDER in support)**
Long pass	**CENTER FORWARD (with WING in support)**

Center mid fielder in possession

During the attacking phase the center mid fielder in possession must place himself diagonally to the defensive player (cf. Figs. 6, 7, 8, 9). This will allow him to receive the ball and to project play into attacking mode.

The center mid fielder might not be placed in the right direction the moment he receives the ball, or he could come under attack from an opponent.

In such cases it is very important to dump on one of the defenders, and the rear section must be ready to move back and give support to their team mate.

Besides getting the ball from the defenders, the center mid fielder can also receive (dumps) from the wing or the inside mid fielder.

Once he has possession, the center mid fielder has the following options open to him:

1. outlet towards the flanks to the side defender on the weak flank.
2. diagonal outlet: pass onto the feet of the wing who keeps himself wide or pass onto the feet of the inside mid fielder who opens out towards the flank as the wing cuts inside.
3. vertical play: to the inside mid fielder who receives and goes with the ball or to the wing who comes in to receive between the opposing defense and mid field lines.
4. long pass: to the striker who comes to meet the ball or who opens out towards the flank.

Clearly then the center mid fielder has many and varied options open to him and it is a good idea to set up predominant flows of play so as to avoid confusion in the team.

In particular, the movements of the inside mid fielder and the wing must be connected. When the center mid fielder is in possession, if the wing comes in, the inside mid fielder must widen out with the double aim of freeing space for the center mid fielder's pass to the wing while at the same time giving width to the team. If, on the other hand, the wing stays close to the sideline, the inside mid fielder must be ready (going forward slightly in diagonal to the center mid fielder) to receive the ball on the inside of the field.

The attacking plays of the 4-3-3 are very likely to come to a standstill if the center mid fielder does not have things clear and if the inside mid fielder and the wing are not able to make coordinated movements.

The playing solutions open to the center mid fielder are set out in Figs. 10 and 11.

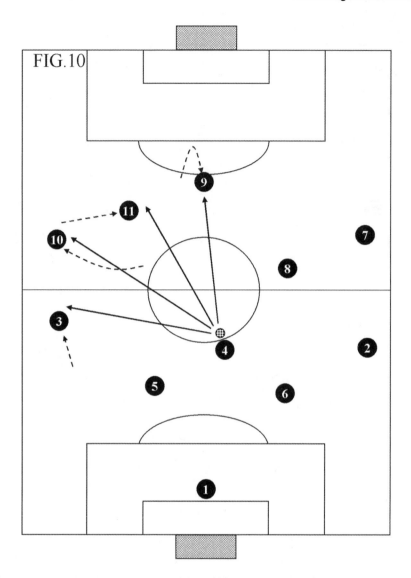

FIG.10

Dumping option (outlet)	**SIDE DEFENDER**
Diagonal option	**INSIDE MID FIELDER**
Vertical option	**WING**
Long pass	**CENTER FORWARD**

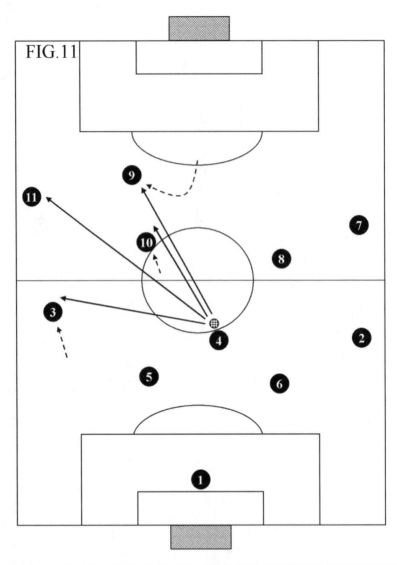

FIG.11

Dumping option (outlet)	**SIDE DEFENDER**
Diagonal option	**WING**
Vertical option	**INSIDE MID FIELDER**
Long pass	**CENTER FORWARD**

In cases where the center mid fielder has decided to open out to the side defender on the weak flank, the receiver will then have all the options open to him which we have already outlined above (cf: Side defender in possession).

If the center mid fielder has played to the wing, the inside mid fielder or the center forward, the team will presumably now be able to start on the consecutive phase of finishing touches.

MAKING THE MOST OF BUILDING UP IN CONSIDERATION OF THE OPPONENTS' TACTICAL MOVES

It goes without saying that the solutions we have set out above are only general directives that the coach must give his team.

It is important, therefore, to perfect your flow of play in consideration of the opponent you are facing.

To give maximum effectiveness to your attacking strategy you must be familiar with all those points of reference that will enable you to outline the tactical behavior of the opponents during the phase of non possession. This will allow you to surprise them and 'play against' them.

The opponents' playing system is the only variable that we will be taking into consideration here, so as to set out a number of typical developments during the build-up phase.

Building up against a 4-4-2.

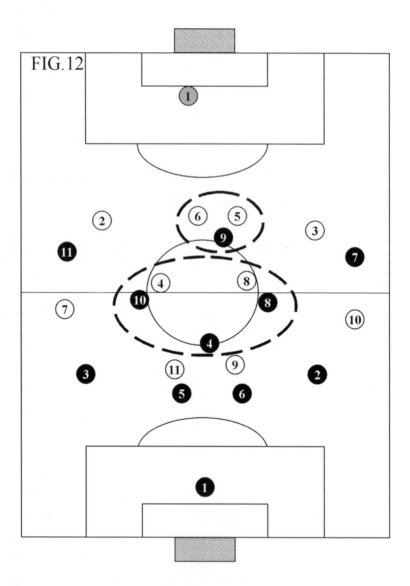

FIG. 12

As we can see in Fig. 12, these are the principle contests that will emerge on the flanks:

- our side defenders are contrasted by the opposing side mid fielders

• our wings will be contrasted by the opposing side defenders

In the center on a level with our defense section, our two backs will have to deal with the opposing pair of strikers.

However, it is in the areas highlighted in the figures that situations are created with unequal numbers of players.

Level with the center circle the two playing systems normally meet 3 against 2 to our advantage, while the two opposing center defenders are in superiority with regard to our single striker.

Keeping this tactical context in mind, it might be useful to bring play out onto the center mid fielder (a player against whom the opponents find it difficult to defend with the right timing), followed by a vertical pass for the inside mid fielder who comes in to receive. As an alternative, if the opposing center mid fielder is blocking play, our center mid fielder can open out onto the wing, who will have time, space and field to receive.

When it comes down to it, once we have regained possession, we need to be good at directing play out on the flanks by finding an opening on the side back or the wing who has moved back. This second option - as shown in Fig. 13 - is helpful when the opponents are using in-depth pressing and it becomes difficult to get the ball to the side back because he is being closed off at once by the opposing side mid fielder.

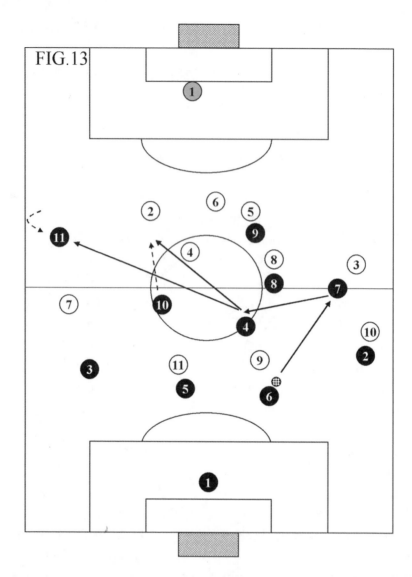

FIG.13

In this case, it is the wing who will have to move back (when a player comes to meet the ball in such a way, the side defender of a section that is using zonal play will find it difficult to antici-pate) and then dump on the center mid fielder, who will develop play on the opponents' weak side.

When the side back on the weak flank does not create the
defense diagonal, tending more to mark the wing than to work in
his team section, it might be a good idea to modify the combination of movements between the wing and the inside mid fielder as
illustrated in Fig. 14.

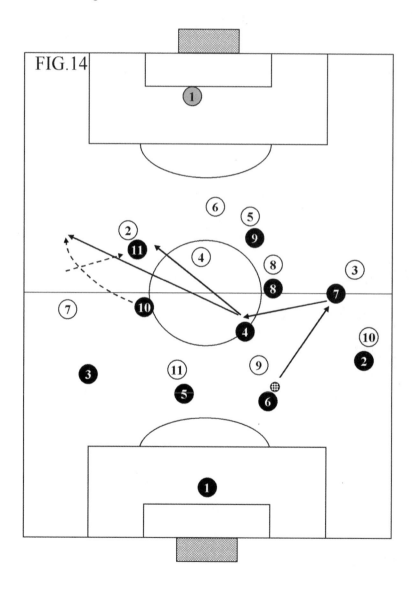

FIG.14

In my opinion, when facing an opponent fielded with the 4-4-2 which makes good use of the numerical superiority of its center defenders against our center forward, it is not easy to play long passes to the striker in the center.

Building up against a 4-3-3.

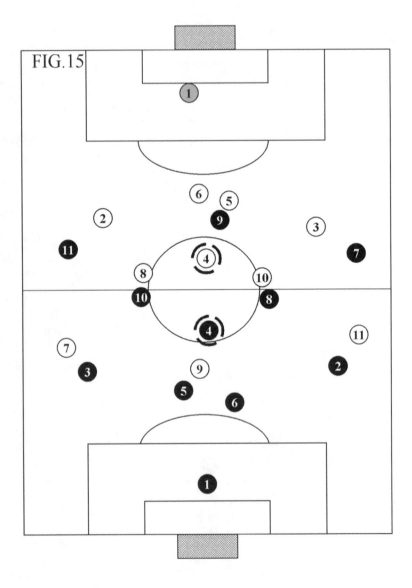

In the tactical contrast between the two systems as shown in Fig. 15, you will see that the two center mid fielders are the players with most space and liberty of action.

On the other hand, it is fairly difficult to get the ball to the center forward, who has two opponents against him.
For this reason, once the defense section has regained possession, it is better to look for a diagonal outlet on the center mid fielder who moves to receive the ball at his feet.

Following on from that, and aiming to bring the ball to the finishing zone, it is better to go for outflanking movements on the sides with combined changes of position.

Making the most of the fact that the opposing side defender will presumably be covering his rival wing, it is possible for us to move our side striker in the direction of the ball so as to create space which the side defender or inside mid fielder will break into as they free themselves of marking along the flanks (cf. Figs. 16, 17 and 18).

In cases where the team is forced to use long passes, it is best to attack the opponents' defense by getting the wing to cut inside to receive the center forward's dump (cf. Fig. 19).

To stop the two opposing center defenders from getting too much of their own way in their 2 to 1 against our center forward, he should free himself of marking on the flank after moving towards the ball.

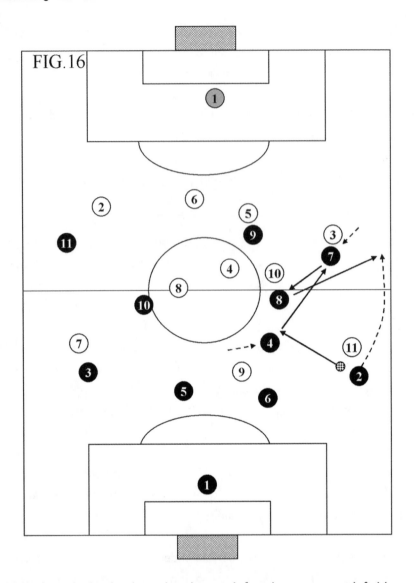

FIG.16

The right side back plays the diagonal for the center mid fielder who has come to meet the ball. The movement develops with a pass towards the wing as he moves to receive the ball, so creating the opportunity for the side defender to break in.

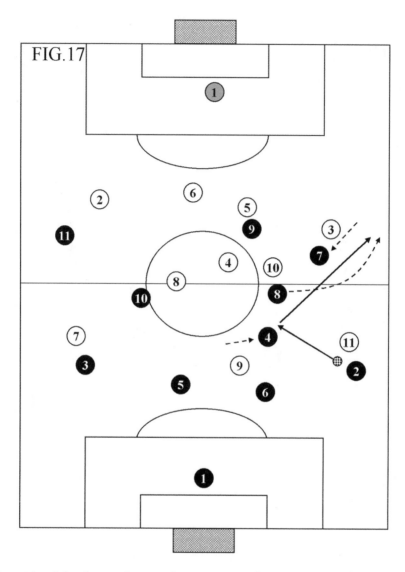

FIG.17

The side defender makes a short pass to the center mid fielder who has come to meet the ball.

Play then develops with a combination of movements between the wing and the inside mid fielder whose job it is to break in along the right flank.

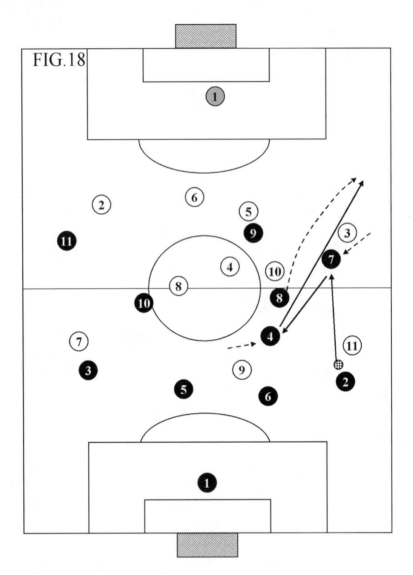

FIG.18

The side defender plays on the feet of the wing, who receives by coming to meet the ball.

Build up develops with a pass from the center to the inside mid fielder, who has set himself up for this along the flanks.

This play can also be carried out with the center defender initially in possession.

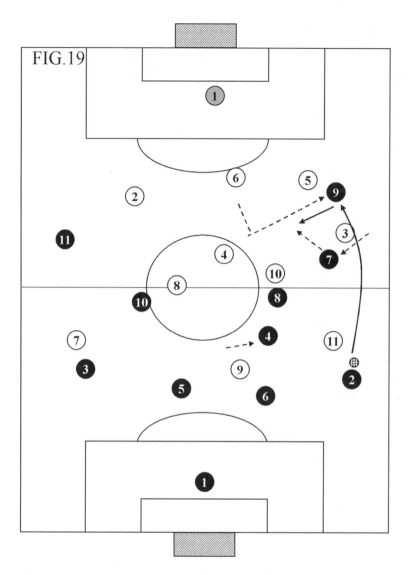

FIG.19

The figure above gives a possible solution when you have opted for a long pass.

The center forward's movement and the wing's cut to the inside must be carried out in cooperation. They are meant as an attack on the zonal defense's classic movements to give coverage (the diagonal and the pyramid).

Building up against a 4-3-1-2.

The diamond-shaped placement of the opponents' mid field puts us in numerical inferiority in the center.
As a consequence, our aim will be to build up play along the flanks.

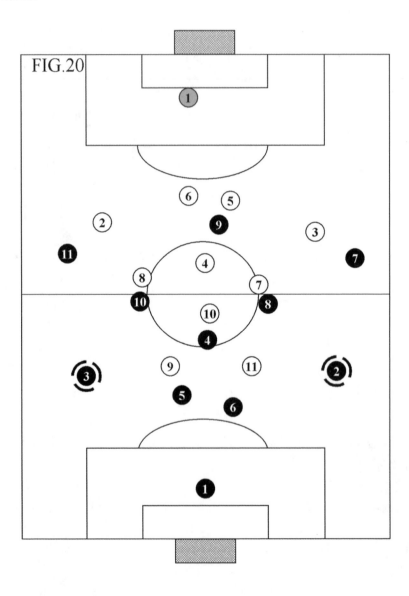

FIG.20

Our team needs to make good, quick use of the time taken by the opponents in shifting back into position in order to give tactical rebalance to the situation along the flanks.

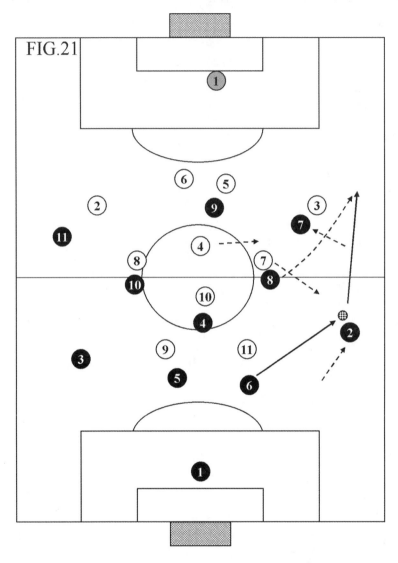

The figure above shows a typical outlet along the flanks, with the side defender receiving as far forward as possible.

Once the side defender is in possession, what we want to do is to block off the classic shifting movement made by the opponents, putting their inside mid fielder along the flank.

You can also attack the sidelines using the wing's inside-outside movements (Fig. 22).

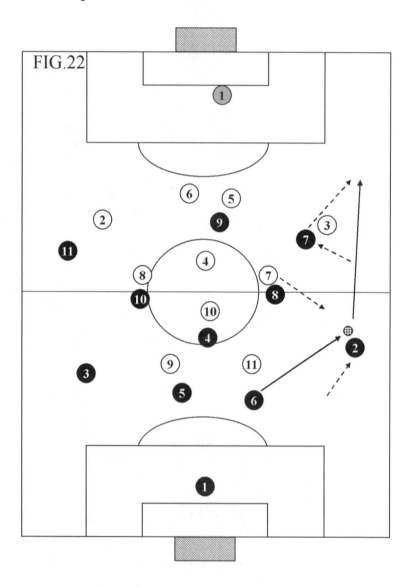

FIG.22

Building up against a 3-4-1-2.

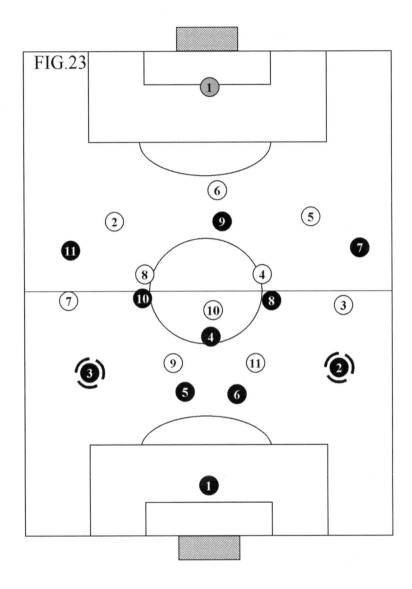

FIG.23

A team fielded with the 3-4-1-2 will probably be using specific measures in their defense phase to make sure that their backs are not playing in numerical equality against the opposing attack.

If that does not happen, i.e., if our opponents have accepted the 3 against 3 situation between our three-man strikers and their opposing defense, then the best thing is to go for long passes so as to set up inside and outside combinations between our strikers.

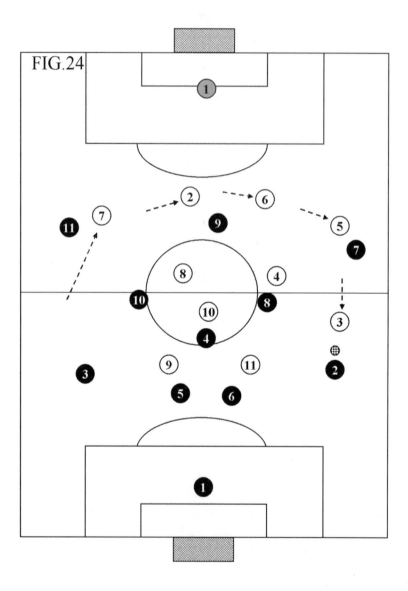

FIG.24

However, our opponents will very probably be using the shifts shown in Fig. 24, trying not to draw on their mid fielders who are face to face with our mid field section.

It goes without saying that we will be able to make a complete study of these shifts only after we have seen the opponents' tactical conduct in action on the field.

In any case, let us imagine that the opponents are fielded and are moving as shown in Fig. 24. One way of making the most of our build up would be:

* outlet on the side defender, who we presume will have the time and space to receive considering his relative distance from the opposing side player.
* Crossover between the wing and the inside mid fielder so as to destabilize the opponents' system of shifts as well as giving the player in possession several options.

Once the maneuver has been set up the side defender in possession can look for the inside mid fielder (Fig. 25) who has broken free along the flanks, or he can pass to the wing who has cut in (Fig. 26).

The ball can reach the wing either directly or indirectly from the center forward's dump.

The inside mid fielder's movement to 'bring away' the opposing center mid fielder is very important as it will allow the side defender to pass the ball to the center forward (or directly to the wing).

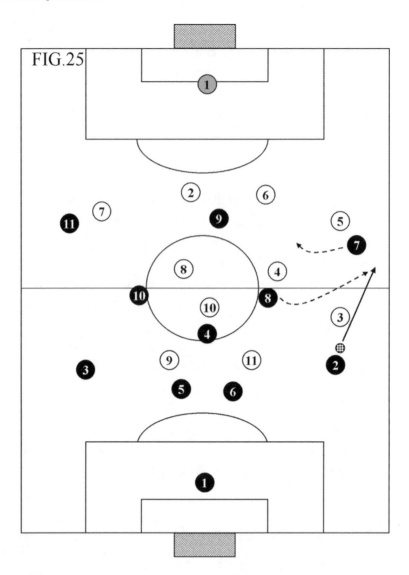

FIG.25

The team creates the situation for finishing touches by exploiting the time it will necessarily take the opponents to shift into the correct positions. The wing 'lunges' into the center of the field and the inside mid fielder uses the space created.

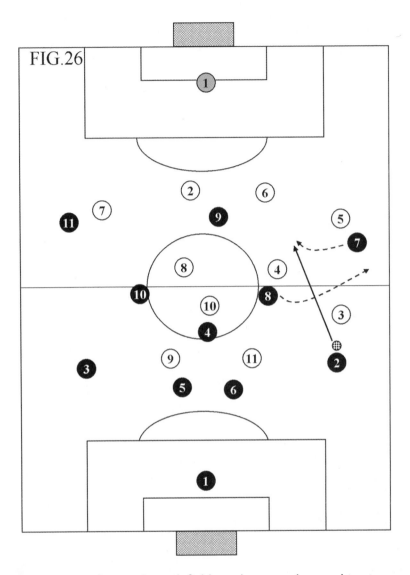

FIG.26

In Fig. 26 it is the inside mid fielder who gets the combination moving. He deviates towards the flanks, setting up the situation for a filtered ball that will allow the side striker to receive near the opposing defense section.

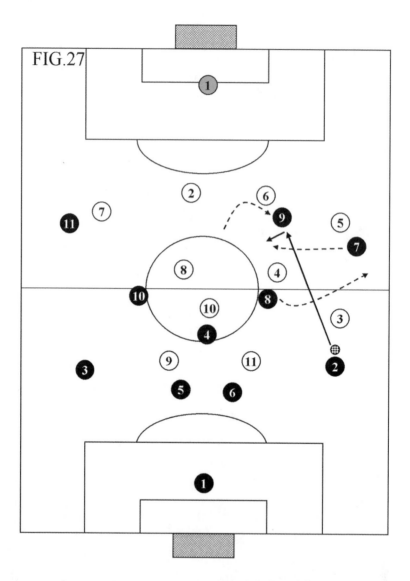

FIG.27

In Fig. 27 the build up is carried out with the help of the center forward.

In this case, you try to get through the opponents' defense by 'forcing' the classical shifting movements of the zonal defense.

Building up against a 5-3-2.

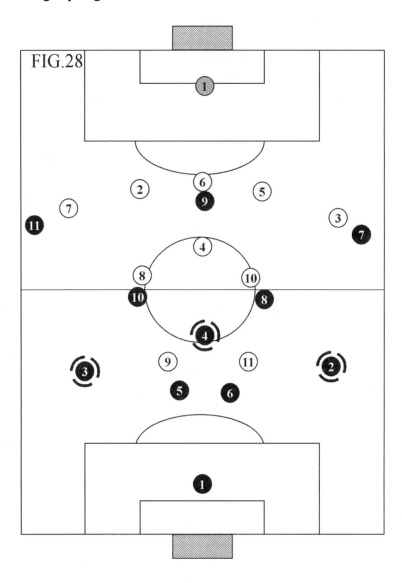

FIG.28

As you can see in the figure above, there are three downfield points of reference to be counted on in launching play.

The opponents' tactical placement goes against vertical play, and it is preferable to use markedly horizontal maneuvers trying to get near their goal by systematically playing onto the weak side.

A flow of play like that shown in Figure 29 is useful to bring the ball up, taking as much advantage as we can of the freedom that the opponents' system is giving to our own side players and the center mid fielder.

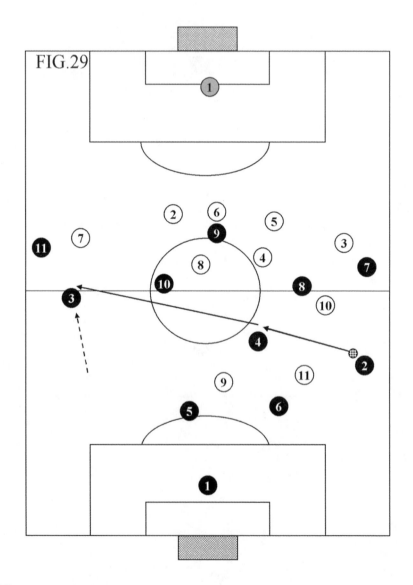

FIG.29

The solutions that we have set out are no more than examples based on possible interpretations of the build up phase in relation to the opponents' collective placement on the field.

It is important to give flow to the team's play in order to regulate collective tactical conduct, but it must also be pointed out that many plays involve the team regaining possession in tactical conditions that are very different from those that we have set out.

It is, for example, quite possible for the mid fielders to regain possession, and they will then find themselves able to attack opponents who are not all placed below the line of the ball.

Coaching the post-conquest sub-phase and the development of breaks are two very important things to be kept in mind and prepared for in the best way possible in connection with the coach's own ideas.

Step No. 8 is entirely dedicated to teaching these aspects of the game.

STEP 3

FINISHING
TOUCHES

Once you are near the opponents' goal, the next thing is to make the best possible use of finishing touches so as to put a player in position to shoot.

From a technical point of view, you can carry out finishing touches by using:

• Crosses
• Dump and rebound passes (as the player breaks in)
• Filtering passes (after cuts)
• Passes after overlapping
• Wall passes after combinations
• Simple passes that make use of the numerical advantage created, for example by good dribbling.

My own studies carried out during the World Cup in France in '98 have allowed me to come up with the following figures:

• 12.85 % of successful finishing touches were carried out in the defensive half.
• 87.15 % of successful finishing touches were carried out in the attacking half.
• 77.83 % of successful finishing touches were carried out in the last 30 meters of the field.

In Fig. 30 I have drawn up one by one the percentages of successful finishing touches in relation to the various parts of the field.

FIG.30

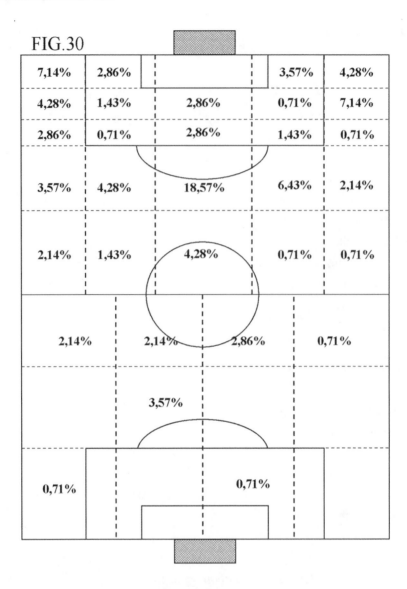

Finishing touches are the combined actions of the player who frees himself of marking and the passer who carries out the assist. It will be clear that the key factors in making sure everything works as smoothly as possible are technical ability and tempo.

From the technical point of view it is essential that the pass is sent in the right direction at the right moment.

The key factor is the distance that separates the player carrying out the finishing touches and the player who is to shoot. The shorter the distance between the goal scorer and the one sending him the ball, the easier it will be from a technical point of view to carry out the pass.

From the point of view of tempo, it is vital for the goal scorer to place himself in the right way to receive the assist the moment his team mate can play it to him (open ball).

Distance has an important role to play as far as timing is concerned as well. The shorter the distance that separates the player who is to shoot from the one giving him the assist, the less time the ball will take to arrive to the possible goal scorer, which will make it more simple for him to calculate more or less when he should free himself of marking in order to pick up the assist.

In my opinion, however, the most important factor for the player who has to free himself of marking is another: the starting signal.

Deciding when to free yourself of marking is absolutely vital when you need to get rid of the defense shield.

The fact that finishing touches take place principally in the last 30 meters is closely connected with the positive outcome of problems concerning distance and starting signals.

Around our opponents' penalty area distances tend to be shortened in, and at the same time it becomes easier to read the situation from a tactical point of view - i.e., to understand that your team mate is about to apply finishing touches.

Solving the enigma: perfecting distance and signals

We have just seen that the nearer the player applying finishing touches is to the possible goal scorer, the easier it will be:

- to carry out the assist from a technical point of view;
- to find the right tempo between the pass and the breaking free of marking.

The first thing that we can say about carrying out successful finishing touches is connected with the moment in which the play is made: the assist must only be executed when the two players are close together. In other words, you apply finishing touches when the two players are placed in nearby sections and when the ball is not far away from the opponents' defense section.

The other factor to be looked at is the signal.
When the ball is near the opponents' defense section, ready for finishing touches to be applied, it is vital that the player who is to shoot chooses to break free of marking the moment the ball is 'open', i.e., in the right conditions to be played.

On the contrary, in cases where the player carrying out finishing touches is under pressure ('closed' ball), there is no point in doing anything to break free of marking other than going to meet the player in possession in order to give him assistance.

SITUATIONAL FINISHING TOUCHES

Just as we have already done as far as building up is concerned, we can classify finishing touches into two groups - situation and schematic.

Our aim is to get past any opposition coming from the opponents' defense section in order to put one of our players in a situation enabling him to shoot.

You can attack the opponents' defense both from the sides (crosses or assists from the side) and centrally.

A central attack can aim to free a player of marking from behind the defense section (using a filtering pass in combination with a cutting movement into space) or in front of it (using a dump and rebound pass, for example, that sets up a shot from outside the area).

Clearly the type of attack you prefer (from the side, centrally from in front or centrally from behind) will depend first of all on the types of strikers you have, but also on the part of the field where the team is playing.

When the opponents' defense section is blocked rigidly in or around its own penalty area there is very little space to attack in depth and it might be more fruitful to try to get through from the sides.
On the contrary, when the opposing defense section is playing at greater depth it will be simpler and more direct to make assists behind the rival backs.

RULES REGARDING GIVING AND READING SIGNALS TO IMPROVE SITUATIONAL FINISHING TOUCHES

Players must be given universal rules so that they can develop effective finishing touches. The signals and the way in which the players read them must be consistent before starting to work on playing tempo.

We can say, basically, that finishing touches are carried out by two 'actors': the player in possession (finisher) and the one - or ones - without the ball (shooter).

In order to make finishing touches really dangerous the player in possession must be able to pass the ball to another player who is freeing himself of marking (open ball condition).

The main signal on the basis of which the shooter will decide whether or not to free himself of marking is the situation of the ball (open ball, playable - closed ball, unplayable).

Rules: playing options and movement connected to the signal.

Player without the ball

Signal: open ball ▷ **interpretation:** free yourself of marking.

Signal: closed ball ▷ **interpretation:** go in support.

In relation to the correct tactical reading by the player without the ball we can now add that of the player in possession, as follows:

Player with the ball

Signal: movement to break free of marking ▷ **interpretation:** play an assist.

Signal: movement in support ▷ **interpretation:** give and go.

Basically, when the player without the ball sees that the player in possession is in a position to play the assist, he will free himself of marking in order to receive it.

On the other hand, when the player in possession is not able to carry out the pass because he is closely pressed, the other breaks free of marking in order to give him assistance or support.
Once he has made his dumping pass, it is vital that the player who was in possession should move into the space in order to make the play more dynamic and to give flow to the 'chain of situational play'.

In Fig. 30 you can see the strikers' clear movement to get free of marking as they break into space having received the signal of open ball.

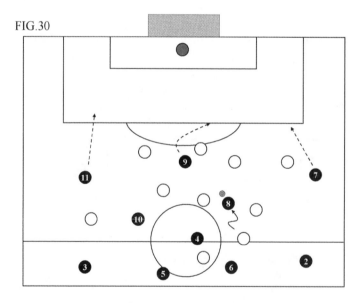

FIG.30

In Fig. 31, on the other hand, the strikers' movements give support to the player in possession when the signal indicates closed ball.

FIG.31

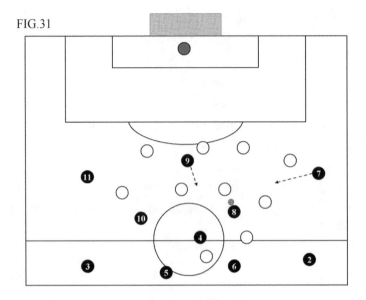

In Fig. 32 (which is a development of the situation in Fig. 30), the player in possession chooses his play (assist) in relation to the movement of the player without the ball.

FIG.32

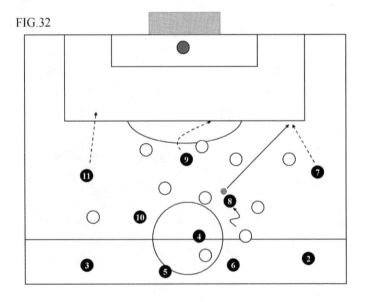

Figures 33 and 34 on the other hand show the correct interpretation (give and go) made by the player in possession to a closed ball situation.

In Fig. 33 (leading on from what we saw in Fig. 31) it is the mid fielder who dumps on the center forward and then breaks into space.

FIG.33

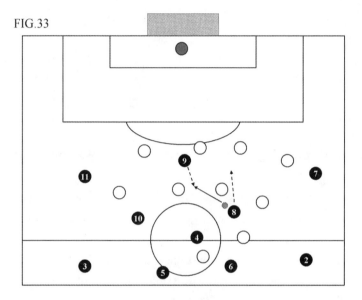

In Fig. 34, the center forward is in a closed ball situation (there are defenders behind him and he cannot therefore turn around to carry out the assist). He dumps on the supporting player and goes straight away to attack depth.

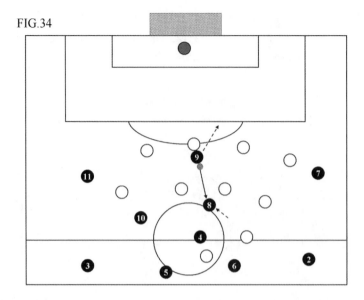

FIG.34

Improving playing time in situational finishing touches.

Once the team understands all the rules, signals and movements, it is essential to show them how to time these things correctly.

Here again, the most important signal associated with the rules about timing play is connected with the situation of the ball (open ball / playable - closed ball / unplayable).

When the ball is closed you get immediate play - i.e., the combined technical and tactical choice of the player in possession (dump and go) and the receiver (movement in to support) must take place at once.

Signal: closed ball ▷ **timing:** ▷ immediate.

With an open ball, the timing - i.e., the combined technical tactical choice of the player in possession (assist) and the receiver (movement to break free of marking) will depend on how much space the player in possession has to play in.

If the field is 'open', the players will delay their combined choice (breaking free of marking + assist) so as to gain space by getting nearer to the goal.

If the field is 'closed' the players will carry out their choices at once.

In practice, if the player in possession has freed himself of his direct marker, or if he is in any case in a position to run in the direction of the opposing goal without coming under contrast, the player without the ball will delay his own movement to break free of marking in order to allow the other to reach a better position to carry out his finishing touches.

SCHEMATIC FINISHING TOUCHES

Schematic finishing touches draw on pre-determined lines of play of great use in getting past the opponent's defense barriers.

The basic signals allowing the various players to move around and set up attacking plays 'with their eyes closed' are connected with the singling out of precise chains of play.

As we have already seen in connection with the build-up sub-phase, what the coach must do is single out possible receivers in relation to the players in possession so that they can make use of:

* a dump (or a long opening)
* at least one solution from the following:
    o a pass into depth;
    o a wall pass;
    o a pass (or dump and rebound) as he breaks into space.

The dump (or the opening pass) is an important option when the opponents are in good control of the zone on the field where our team is developing play, and the player in possession thinks it best to look for alternative ways of getting through.

The other solutions (pass into depth or filter, wall pass, simple pass or dump and rebound as a team mate breaks into space) are all good ways of leading up to well identified finishing touch plays (cuts, combination, overlapping, dump and rebounds).

Central penetration

In what follows, we will outline some of the possible solutions for a player in possession and the coordinated movements of the various members of the chain formed by the inside mid fielder - the wing - the center forward.

The inside mid fielder in possession.

When he is in possession the inside mid fielder has the following options of play:

Dumping option	**CENTER MID FIELDER**
Opening option	**WING (ON THE WEAK SIDE)**
Vertical option	**WING (ON THE STRONG SIDE)**
Vertical option	**CENTER FORWARD**

Vertical options are useful both for making long passes into depth (filtering passes) and for playing the wall pass.
When the team has space in front, what you will be trying to do is hit the opponents' defense from behind and in cases such as these the strikers will move to receive the pass in the open spaces.

If the opposing defense is lined up on the edge of its own penalty area, the inside mid fielder will go to make use of a pass rebounding from one of the strikers who will act as a wall sending the pass back to the mid fielder after he has broken into space.

In the following figures we try to illustrate some of the typical developments of play with the inside mid fielder in possession.

FIG.35

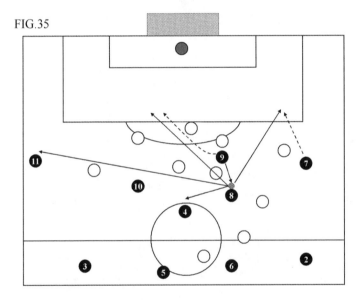

The inside mid fielder receives the center forwards dump and can choose between:

* an in depth pass towards the wing
* an in depth pass on the center forward, who sprints towards it after the dump
* opening to the wing on the weak side
* dump on the center mid fielder

Coaching the 4-3-3

Solutions that are roughly similar are shown in figures 36 and 37. In the first case the inside mid fielder receives the dump from the wing and follows by going to carry out finishing touches. In the second case, it is the center mid fielder who passes to his team mate on the inside.

FIG.36

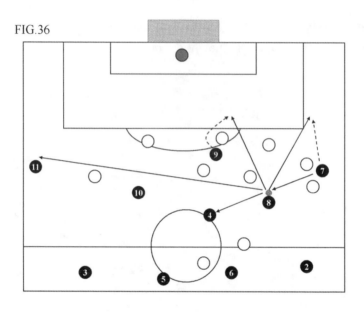

FIG.37

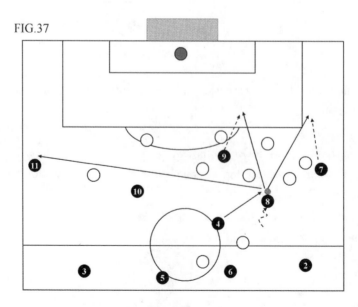

When the wing or the center forward do not have enough space to attack in depth, their movements to come and meet him will give the inside mid fielder the chance to try to get past the opponents' defense section by using a combination.

There is an example of this in figure 38. The inside mid fielder goes for a combination with the center forward after having received the wing's dump.

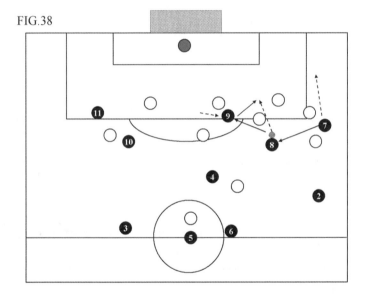

FIG.38

In figure 39 we show a combination between inside mid fielder - wing - inside mid fielder, which will take place after a dump from the center forward.

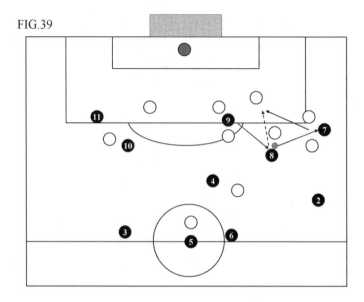

FIG.39

Wing in possession

The typical playing options for the side attacking player are:

Dumping option	**INSIDE MID FIELDER**
Opening option	**INSIDE MID FIELDER (ON THE WEAK SIDE)**
Vertical option	**CENTER FORWARD**
Vertical option	**WING (ON THE WEAK SIDE)**

In figure 40 the wing receives a vertical pass from the side mid fielder after having made a counter movement going in. At this point he will have the finishing touch options already shown in the preceding Fig. 39.

FIG.40

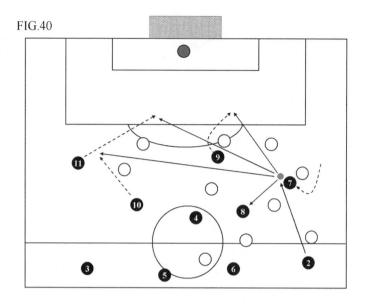

Figures 41 and 42 show the typical wing - center forward - combinations on the flanks and on the inside.

FIG.41

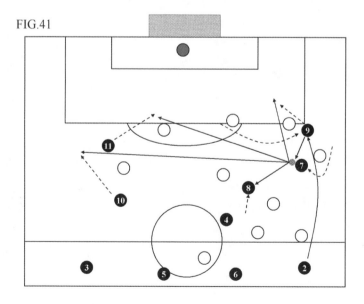

FIG.42

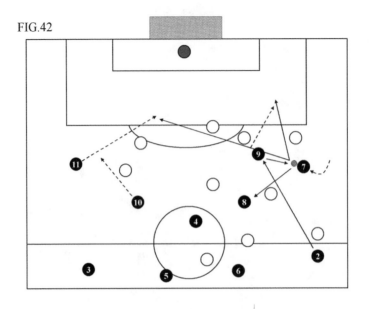

FIG.43

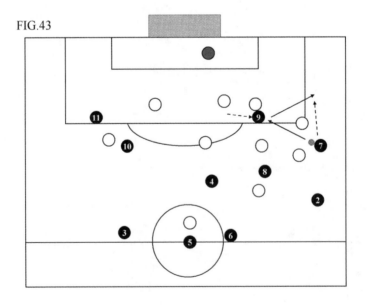

FIG.44

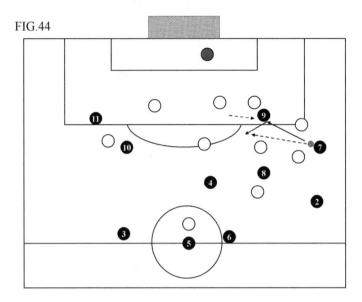

We will finish off this illustration of the playing options open to the wing by pinpointing the solutions facing the attacking side player in cases where he receives the ball from the inside mid fielder on the weak side.

Here the wing will not have the opportunities given to him by the inside mid fielder - center forward - wing chain, but those we will be looking at when we speak about the penetration along the flanks provided to him by the wing - inside mid fielder - side defender chain.

A typical example is set out below. Once the wing has received the ball and made sure that conditions are not right to make an attack personally with the ball at his feet, he will dump on the inside mid fielder and offer himself in depth.

As shown in the figure, the inside mid fielder can play a filter to the wing or pass to the side defender as he breaks into the space freed by the movement of the inside mid fielder.

FIG.45

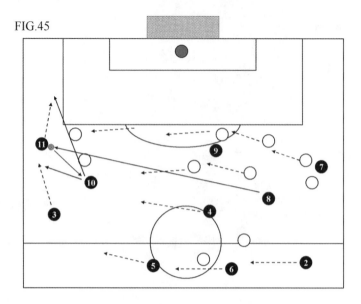

Center forward in possession

In the finishing touch phase, the classic options on hand to the center striker are the following:

Dumping option	**INSIDE MID FIELDER or WING**
Opening option	**INSIDE MID FIELDER or WING (ON THE WEAK SIDE)**
Vertical option	**WING**
Vertical option	**INSIDE MID FIELDER**

The typical finishing touches carried out by the center forward see him act at the top in the role of the player who dumps on his team mates (cf. Fig. 46).

FIG.46

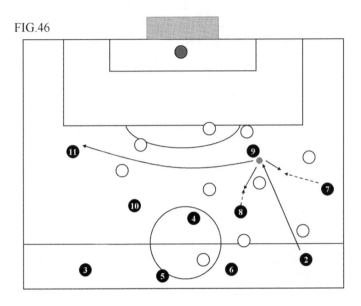

It is possible, however, if the center forward is particularly good at aerial play or if he is very active in creating space by coming to receive diagonal passes between the opponents' defense or mid field lines, that he can also send his team mates into depth as shown in figures 47 and 48 and described in the relative table.

FIG.47

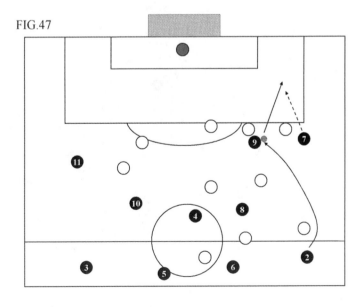

Figure 47 shows the center forward receiving a long pass from the side back. By jumping higher, he is able to anticipate the defender and head the ball beyond the defense line, setting up the wing's break into depth.

Figure 48, on the other hand, shows the center forward receiving a pass between the opponents' lines, and, having controlled the ball, he will filter it towards the right inside mid fielder who is breaking into the free space.

These two typical examples show how it is possible to make use of particular characteristics of the center striker so that he can act as a finishing touch player.

FIG.48

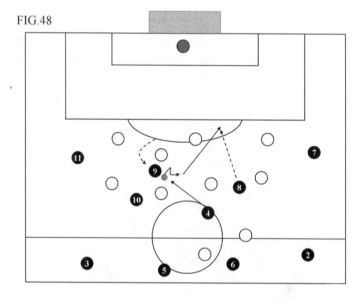

Penetration along the flanks

While the chains formed by the inside midfielder, wing and center forward help to develop mainly central finishing touches, the side chains made up of the side back - inside mid fielder - wing create finishing touches along the flanks ending up with a cross.

The chain formed by the side defender, inside mid fielder and wing can break through on the sides by using combinations both with the ball and without the ball.

In some circumstances it can be useful to develop plays with the side chain that will include one or two central points of reference (the center forward or the center mid fielder).

In the following figures we will be showing some of the classic developments along the sides that can be set up with the 4-3-3.

FIG.49

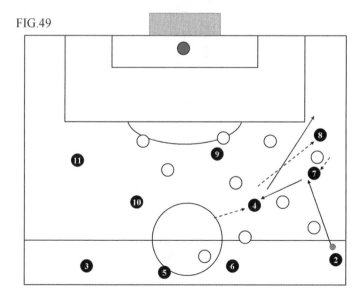

With the side defender in possession, the wing comes to meet him, receiving the ball and freeing the flank which will be occupied by the inside mid fielder.

Figure 50 shows the classic 'dump and go' play carried out by the wing and the inside mid fielder.

FIG.50

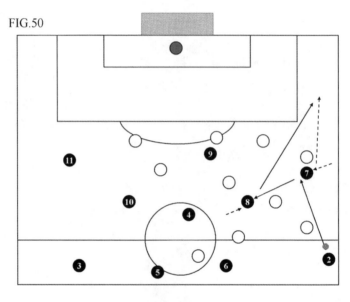

FIG.51

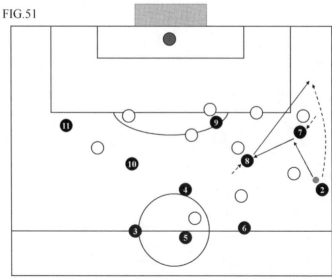

Figure 51 shows the typical combination of the side chain. The side back dumps on the wing and begins to overlap. The wing dumps on the inside mid fielder, who then sends the ball to the inside mid fielder who has broken in and is ready for the cross.

Figure 52 shows a combination of movements without the ball between the wing and the inside mid fielder. The two players cross over so that they can offer the side back two playing options. He can pass to the inside mid fielder along the flank (as shown in the figure) or to the wing 'inside the field'.

FIG.52

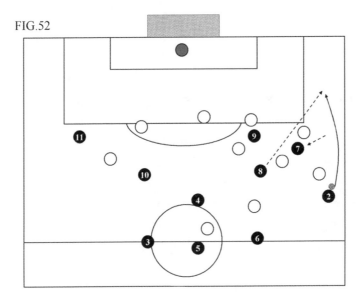

Figure 53 shows the side defender breaking into space following on a change of front. The center mid fielder looks for width, sending the ball to the wing. In combination with the inside mid fielder the side striker puts the side back in a position to cross.

FIG.53

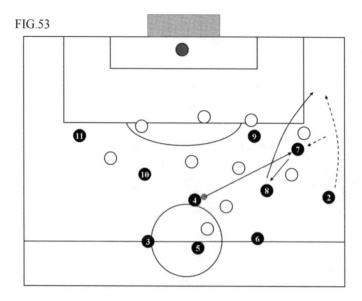

Schemes and playing tempo.

A scheme of play will only be effective and decisive if the players who are setting it up get the tempo and coordination right.

The players will only manage to time their moves if the scheme contains signals which establish the exact moment to start the movements to break free of marking and to make the assist.

However, we must first of all underline how important it is to keep the players and the team sections at the correct distance from each other so as to perfect the players' timing.

When looking at situational finishing touches, we saw that the receiver should break free of marking only when the player in possession is in a condition to carry out the assist (open ball). It goes without saying that the same rule applies when trying to make the best of schematic finishing touches!!!

You often get open ball conditions when making dumps. Looking at the figure below, you can see how the right wing n. 7) times his breaking in movement on the basis of the center forward's (n. 9) back pass towards the right inside mid fielder (n. 8).

FIG.54

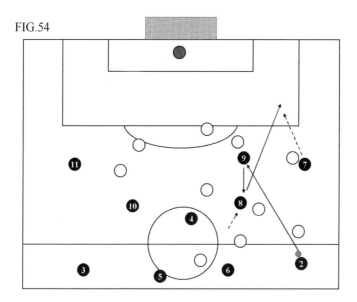

You need to use one touch play when the ball is near the opponents' defense section because that will make it easier to pinpoint the exact moment when the receiver is to get free of marking.
If, after having received the ball from the center forward, the right inside mid fielder (n. 8) had decided to keep it at his feet rather than play it one touch, it would have been that much more difficult for the right wing (n. 7) to decide exactly when to move quickly into depth.

This more difficult 'tactical reading' of the situation might even have made the wing decide not to break free of marking, the extremely negative result of which is that he would no longer be an option for the pass setting him up for finishing touches.

Coaching the 4-3-3

It is therefore, in my opinion, better to 'complicate' the striker's (or the mid fielder's) life when he is in possession by forcing him to use one touch play when near the opponents' defense line rather than allowing him to deal with the ball as he wishes, which stops his team mate who needs to break free of marking from doing so at the right moment.

The risk in the first case is to bungle a couple of passes. In the second case, you might even end up paralyzing all attacking play.

STEP 4

ADAPTING TO THE ATTACKING PHASE

Looking carefully at the range of options that can be used by the 4-3-3, the first thing you notice is how many developments this system offers and how varied they are.

In reference to all these possibilities, the coach must be well able to pinpoint his players' main characteristics and tailor make the best solutions for them.

I have read interviews with leading coaches who declare that their team is not cut out to interpret a certain system rather than another.

My opinion is that any professional group of 20 / 25 players can more or less naturally interpret any system of play if the coach is willing to teach them how to do so and above all if he is able to foresee the best solutions in relation to the quality of his players.

Having now underlined what in my opinion is an important point, I will have a look at some of the typical developments of the 4-3-3.

The 4-3-3 of the Dutch school.

In the classic 4-3-3 applied by the Dutch teams the three strikers occupy the whole width of the opponents' front.

The wings play 'with their feet on the line'; using elaborate build up, the team tries to break through principally on the flanks so as to create finishing touch conditions using crosses.

Two particularly used themes are the attempt to change front (cf. Fig. 55) and the overlapping of the side back.

FIG.55

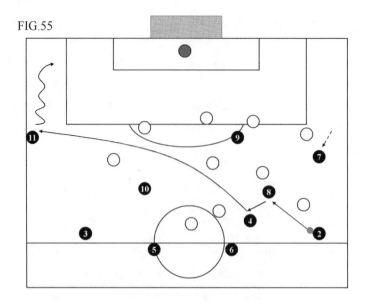

Breaking though in the center comes about principally by using combinations between the inside mid fielder and the center forward.

FIG.56

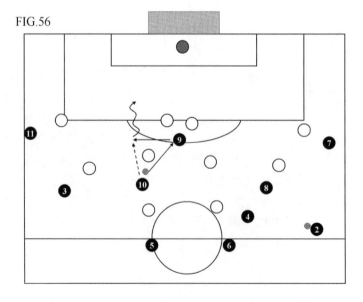

The 4-3-3 developed vertically.

The vertical development of maneuvers sees the three strikers placed quite closely together.

The center forward usually acts as an advanced hinge and the wings are ready to attack space to receive the dumps (having made the classic crisscross movement) or to receive balls nicked into depth.

Build-up is carried out with little elaboration or useless embellishments and finishes up principally on the strikers, who attack the opponents' backs using rapid combinations in order to free a man either behind the opposing defense section (cf. Fig. 57) or in front of it (for a shot from outside the area).

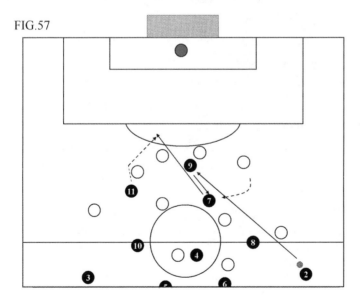

FIG.57

When the maneuver needs to be widened out on the flanks to attack a solid defense, play will be organized by the inside mid fielders with well-timed movements of deviation, or by the side backs with vertical break-ins.

The principle characteristics of the single players in interpreting the 'Dutch' 4-3-3.

Side back: he must be good at sprinting up, have tempo and be able to carry out good crosses.

Center mid fielder: good vision of play, able to change attacking front with good effect.

Inside mid fielder: good at managing the ball in tight situations and at breaking in vertically. Good shot from far out.

Center forward: good at combinations with team mates in tight situations, good aerial play and in attacking crosses.

The principal characteristics of the single players in interpreting the 4-3-3 developed vertically.

Side back: good at running both with the ball and without, ability to make effective crosses.

Center mid fielder: good at blocking and getting the maneuver to start up again with speed.

Inside mid fielder: all-around player who participates actively in the defense phase and is able to carry out dangerous breaks along the flanks in attacking situations.

Wing: good at filtering balls and at receiving in open space. Able to shoot both from outside the area and as he runs towards the goal.

Center forward: very good when acting as a buoy, good aerial play, able to make combinations with his team mates.

STEP 5

GETTING THE
ATTACKING
PHASE ACROSS

Having set out the principles and the attacking developments of the 4-3-3, the moment has now arrived to get on the field and get things across to the team.

Teaching the attacking and defending phases means getting the team to develop their abilities going from the learning phase right on up to the action (or execution) phase.

During the learning phase, the players' mental processes will first of all break up - in ways that will be more or less evident, depending on the technical or intellectual ability of the group - the various elements that they have to assimilate. These will then grad- ually pilot the team towards those perfectly operational collective reflexes that no longer call for great concentration in order to be put into effect.

The player's attention needs to be moved away from the percep- tion and resolution of the actions that concern him alone (for example, how to free himself of his direct opponent) so that in time he will be able to move and behave in such a way as to carry out the pre-established aims of the whole team.

Only when the team has acquired the ability to move and work towards the aims that the various attacking sub phases require of him, will the time have arrived to put opponents on the field, forc- ing each player to move and develop play in consideration of:
      1. the flow of play that has been learned
      2. the way the opponents work against that

We will not be underlining here the technical exercises that can improve those qualities that are of most use to individual players in developing the attacking phase. We will concentrate our attention, instead, on overall or specific exercises (in one or more phases) in order to delineate a possible course of instruction.

One phase exercises for training the building-up sub-phase.

1. *Moving the ball around inside the defense section without opponents' resistance*

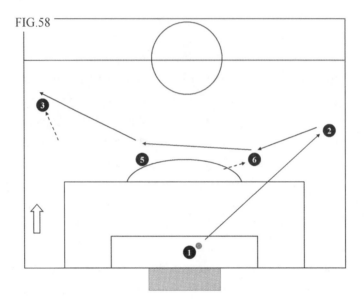

FIG.58

The defense section, made up of 4 players, is placed in and around the penalty area as they pass the ball to each other from right to left and vice versa. When the ball arrives to a side defender, he brings it forward a couple of meters before dumping it on the nearest center defender, who proceeds with the passing towards the other side of the field.

N.B. for reasons of space, Fig. 58 shows only one series of passes.

2. Moving the ball around inside the defense section with the resistance of 2 opponents

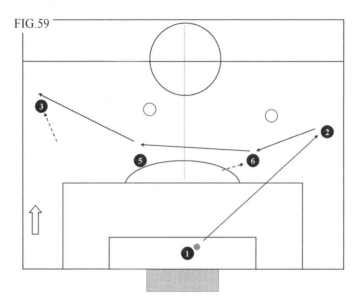

FIG.59

This exercise is very similar to the preceding one. The only differ-ence is that the 2 opponents, who can only intervene in their own sector, stop the defense section from moving up as they pass the ball around.

3. Moving the ball around inside the defense section with the resistance of 3 opponents and the help of the center mid fielder

This exercise is similar to the last, with the difference that a low lying point of reference (the center mid fielder) has now been placed on the field as well as an opponent who can go anywhere he wants (the player with the gray tunic).The other two opponents can still only contrast in their own sectors.

The aim of the four defenders, aided by the center mid fielder, is to bring the ball over the mid field line without any player ever advancing vertically with the ball for more than 5 meters.

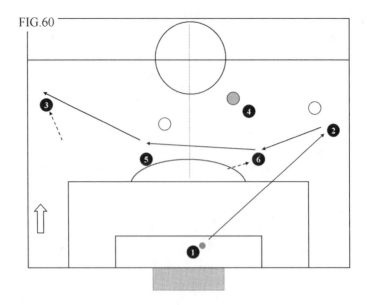

FIG.60

A couple of possible developments are shown in the following figures.

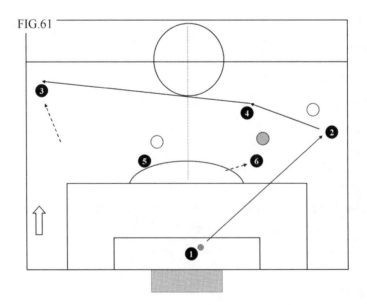

FIG.61

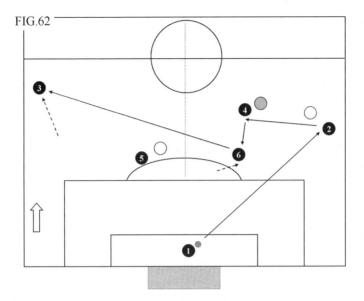

4. Moving the ball around inside the defense and mid field sections without opponents' resistance

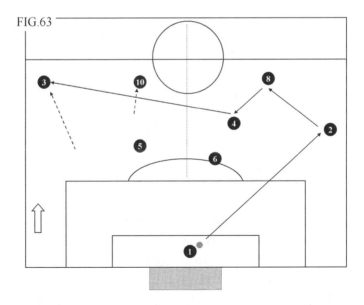

The defense and mid field sections are lined up in this exercise. The aim is to develop play on the weak side sending the ball between the sections by using diagonal passes.

5. *Moving the ball around inside the defense and mid field sections with the resistance of 5 opponents*

In this exercise the defense and mid field sections are trying to bring the ball over the mid field line.

They are being obstructed by 4 opponents (2 for each section) in white tunics + 1 player (in the gray tunic) who is free to move about wherever he wants.

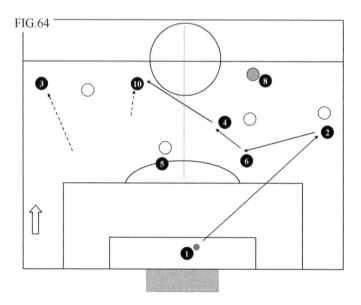

FIG.64

6. *Moving the ball around inside the sections (11 against 0)*

The entire team lines up on the whole field and interacts without resistance from opponents. The aim is to get the ball to a player (inside mid fielder, wing or side defender) who is in a position to carry out finishing touches (near the hypothetical opponents' defense line) by developing maneuvers that put the three rules of situational build-up into effect.
In cases where build-up is carried out using schemes you tell the team to execute them.

7. Moving the ball around inside the sections with the resistance of 7 opponents

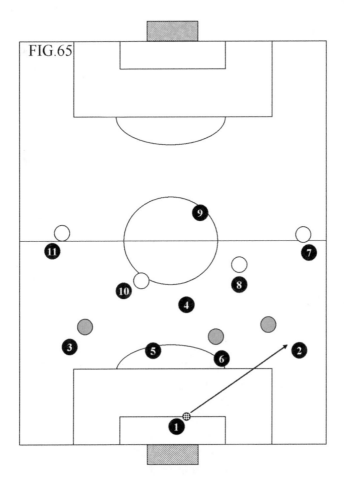

FIG.65

The team has the same aim as in the preceding exercise. 3 opponents in gray tunics are placed on the field and their job is to put pressure on the defenders and expose the center mid fielder, and 4 other opponents in white who mark the inside mid fielders and the wings man to man and can intervene on passés towards the center forward.

8. Moving the ball around inside the sections against 8 opponents

This develops in exactly the same way as the last exercise. However, a new defender has been put on the field against the opposing center forward (forcing the team, basically, to go for diagonal outlets on the center mid fielder who is still free) and then against the opposing center mid fielder (forcing the team to go for long passes to the center forward who is free).

9. Moving the ball around inside the sections against 9 opponents

The development of this exercise for the build-up phase is the same as the last one. In this exercise, however, both the center mid fielder and the center forward are marked by an opponent.

10. Moving the ball around inside the sections against 10 opponents (keeper excluded)

The team's aim is to develop play so as to bring the ball to a player placed near the opponents' defense section who will be able to carry out finishing touches.

It is possible to use this exercise in sessions to prepare an upcoming match, fielding the team acting as the sparring-partner with the playing system that the opponents will probably be using.
The coach will give indications and will make the team carry out the best flows of play to get past the opponents' attacking and mid field sections.

Single phase exercises to coach the finishing touches sub-phase

Instruction on the finishing touches phase begins by developing possible combinations to be carried out by the three-man attack and goes on to involve the two inside mid fielders and then the center mid fielder and the defenders.

It is a good idea to consider doing some specific work on various chains of play.

1. Combinations with the attacking chain (wing - center forward - wing)

The three players placed at different levels on the field (i.e., near the opponents' goal), are asked to develop combinations which will permit them to shoot after having made cuts into depth or zigzag movements away from the flanks.

The first solution will be used chiefly when the three-man attack is placed further back and has space to attack in front. The second prospect will be carried out when the players are positioned near the penalty area. The exercise requires first touch play and will be started off by the coach passing to one of the three strikers.

The following figures show some typical developments.

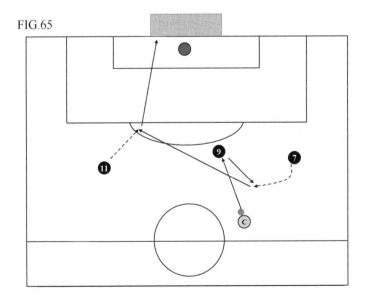

FIG.65

FIG.66

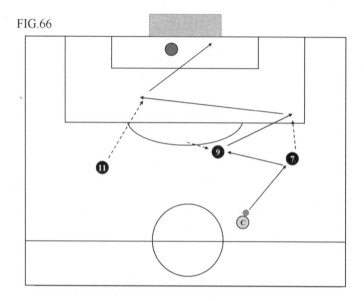

2. Combinations with the attacking chain (wing - center forward - inside mid fielder)

FIG.67

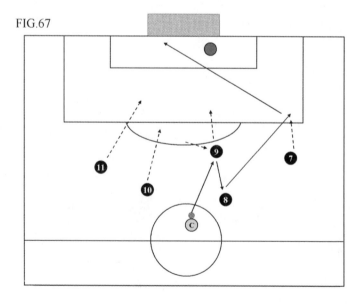

You add the two inside mid fielders to the three-man attack. Without any opposition, the 5 players develop possible finishing touches connected with the system. A typical example can be seen in figure 67.

When the players have got hold of the movements and the playing tempo, making first touch passes all the time, various defenders will be placed on the field until you get a situation of 5 vs 5.

3. Combinations with the side chain (wing - inside mid fielder - side defender)

To the 5 players already in use, we now add the two side mid fielders and the center mid fielder. The n. 8's job is to get to finishing touches by using side chain combinations.
To begin with, the exercise is carried out without any kind of opposition.
Once the players have acquired the movements and the timing of the plays, the opponents' defense section is fielded followed by the mid field (cf. Fig. 68).

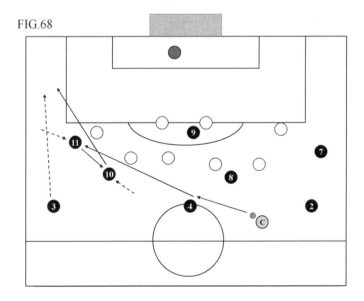

FIG.68

4. Actions on variable themes at different levels on the field.

The eight players in use up to now attack the opponents systematically (7 or 8 of them, depending on the tactical system in use by the team we will be meeting in the next match) placed on two different lines of the field (cf. Fig. 69)

Basically, at the end of every action, while the members of the 4-3-3 are returning to the center of the field, the coach, who has various balls on hand, tells the defenders at what height to place themselves, after which he gives the ball to one of the numbered players as in the figure. The attacking team has to develop incisive actions using mainly first touch play and deciding to go for side or vertical chains, depending on the position of the opposing team. In relation to that, the finishing touch techniques will need to be changed as well.

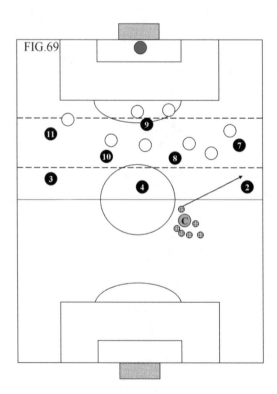

5. Actions on variable themes at different levels on the field.

This exercise is very similar to the last and can be used by coaches who prefer to adopt situational finishing touches rather than schemes.

In the attacking half of the field, the team that is attacking (made up of 8 players: 2 side backs, 1 center mid fielder, 2 inside mid fielders 2 wings and 1 center forward) must get past the opposition of 8 defenders using the 'rules' of situational finishing touches.

6. Training match on variable themes

You play 11 against 11 on the whole field (or with a smaller number of players on a reduced field).

The coach explains to one or both teams which of the various types of build-up and finishing touch techniques they are to use to get into shooting position.

GLOBAL exercise in acquisition of attacking schemes

The coach fields 11 players in the 4-3-3 system.

Instruction begins with the coach indicating 3 defense outlets (dump outlet, diagonal outlet and vertical outlet) to each member of the defense section.

It is important for the moment not to give the long pass as an option.

At this point, the coach indicates the movements to be made by the mid fielders connected with the development of play carried out by the defenders. The aim is to start off from the back section and to end up by moving the ball to the mid field.

The coach will then explain the options of play open to the mid fielders and the connected movements of the players without the ball.

Coaching the 4-3-3

The team is required to carry out flows of play on the field so as to bring the ball into a finishing touch situation.

When the players understand the rules about how to build up play, we will go on to focus our attention on finishing touches.

The coach will list the main solutions open to the player in possession and the movements that the possible receivers have to carry out.

New finishing touch options will be introduced gradually so as not to create confusion in the team.

When the team has learned all the themes connected with elaborate build-up and the possible finishing touch techniques, the coach will then begin to instruct the players on different ways of interpreting long build-up.

STEP 6

POSITIONING DURING THE DEFENSE PHASE

Your interpretation of the defense phase will depend on many things, such as for example: the opponents' tactical system, the ongoing result, the physical condition of the team, etc.

It is vital for the team to be clear about what the coach has in mind and his rules about getting back possession.

In general we can say that a good defense opposition starts off with the work of the strikers and the mid fielders.
It is their job, in fact, to limit the opponents' playing options in their build-up phase.
If the strikers and mid fielders work effectively together they will force the opponents to bring the ball out in conditions that are not perfect for them, so limiting the various finishing touch opportunities open to them.

In defining the collective tactical behavior during the non-possession phase it is a good idea to proceed in the following way:

1. decide what movements the strikers, mid fielders and defenders should be making to put pressure on the opponents' defense section when it is in possession.
2. decide on the tactical conduct to be adopted (forcing, moving backwards, doubling up) when the ball is on a level with the opponents' mid field section.
3. define the defenders' and mid fielders' movements (coming out to put under pressure, covering and doubling up) and their tactical conduct when the opponents are maneuvering the ball in front of our own defense section.

Now we will look at various lines of conduct to be put to use depending on the opponents' tactical set up.

ATTACKING PLAYERS' AND MID FIELDERS' MOVEMENTS TO COME OUT AND PUT ON THE PRESSURE.

4-3-3 against 4-4-2.

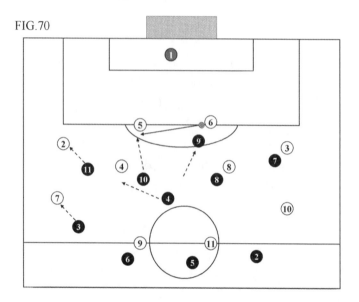

FIG. 70

The fact that we have only one striker gives us the problem of moving a player when the ball is being played by the center defenders of a four-man defense.

In cases where we are meeting a 4-4-2, the movements to create pressure can be the ones shown in the figure.
The wings keep wide on the defenders and it is the inside mid fielder who must come up to put pressure on the opponent in possession as the center mid fielder goes to close off the opponent left free by the n. 10.

FIG.71

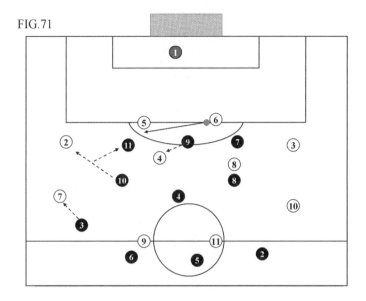

Figure 71 shows an example of how to defend when the opponents' defense section is in possession in cases where we have opted to keep our wings 'tight'.

The three attacking players have the job of closing on the two center defenders and of putting both the center mid fielder and the side back on the weak side in the shadow zone.

The inside mid fielder (n. 10 in the figure) goes to the side back on the strong side with the center mid fielder shielding in front of the defense and shortening in on the opposing center mid fielder (n. 4 in the example) in cases where he comes forward.

4-3-3 against 4-3-3.

FIG.72

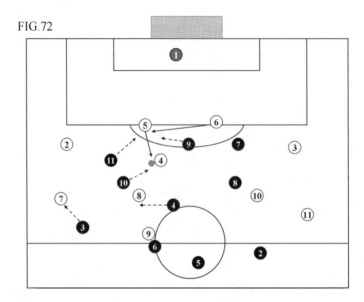

Pressing a team fielded with the 4-3-3 means wiping out the numerical superiority of the central defenders against the center of our attack while at the same time cutting out the opposing low lying center mid fielder.

In figure 72, our left wing n. 11 goes to put pressure on the opponents' defense player n. 5 while our n. 10 shortens up on the opposing center mid fielder, n. 4. It is very important that in carrying out this movement n. 11 tries to close off the direction of the opposing center defender's (n. 5) pass to the right side back (n. 2).

In cases where 5 manages to pass to 2, our left inside mid fielder (n. 10) moves out on the flank while the center mid fielder (n. 4) goes to put pressure on the opponents' inside mid fielder (n. 8) and our two attacking players (n. 9 and 11) put the opponents' n. 4 and 5 into the shadow zone. (cf. Fig. 73)

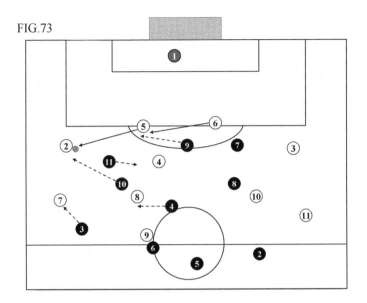

FIG.73

4-3-3 against 4-3-1-2.

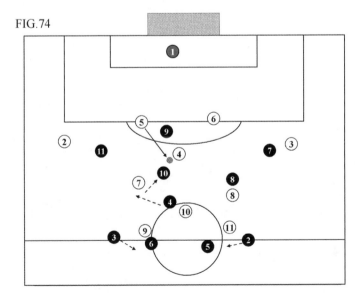

FIG.74

The situation of numerical inferiority in the central area (both on a level with the defense section and in the middle of the field) will not allow us to be aggressive against the center opponents without running risks.

It is difficult to make our defense section's numerical superiority count against the opponents' two strikers when the ball is in the control of the rival's defense section.

The situation is better when the opposing center mid fielder is in possession. In such cases we can bring the nearest inside mid fielder immediately out while the center mid fielder moves forward and the opponents' three-quarter area is left to the defense section.

4-3-3 against 3-4-1-2.

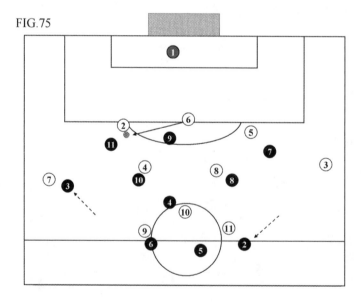

FIG.75

When meeting the 3-4-1-2 it is important to have a close look at the position of the opponents' side players. If they usually receive the ball in depth you can carry out the shift shown in Fig. 75.

The side defenders shift heavily while the attacking players close off the center and the mid fielders find themselves quite naturally on their opposing points of reference.

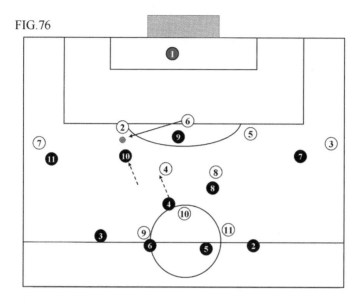

FIG.76

If the opposing side players act as defenders along the flanks, practically changing the opponents' rearguard into a 5-man defense - then our wings keep wide and the mid fielders shift in to the interior (Fig. 76).

4-3-3 against 5-3-2.

Meeting the 5-3-2 we will have the same type of problems that we have already come up against when looking at counter positioning against the 4-3-1-2.

Our numerical inferiority (5 against 3) on a level with the opponents' defense section and the difficulty we have in closing off the low-lying center mid fielder will make it difficult for us to carry out shifts in order to go into so-called ultra-offensive pressing.

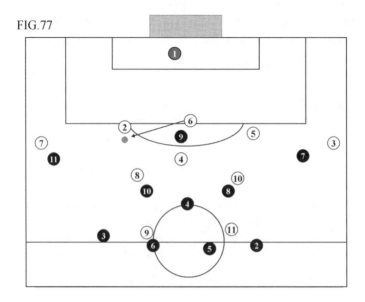

FIG.77

It is easier to manage the tactical situation when the center mid fielder is in possession.

When the wings follow the opponents' side players we can carry out the shifts shown in Fig. 78 in order to put pressure on the player in possession.

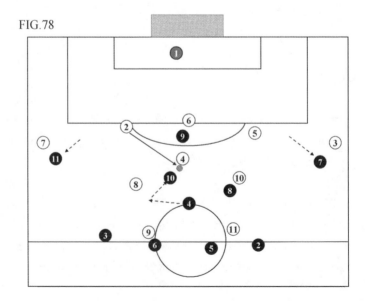

FIG.78

THE DEFENDERS' AND THE MID FIELDERS' STRATEGIC CONDUCT

Having now had a look at some possible solutions when the ball is controlled by the opposing defense section, I will at this point move on to show the tactical conduct to be used when the player in possession is level with our defense section.

This situation comes about when the opponents have got past the barrier formed by our attackers and mid fielders.
In such situations it is necessary to instruct the players who have remained above the line of the ball on how to get back into a useful position, giving them indications on where to place themselves so as to assist the development of a possible break.

4-3-3 against 4-4-2

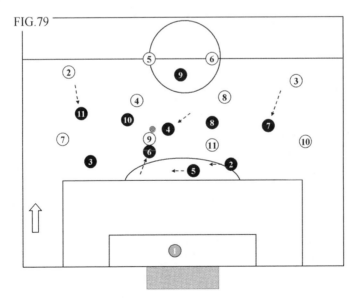

FIG.79

When facing an opponent fielded with the 4-4-2 it is a good idea to use the center mid fielder (who filters and doubles up) as a shield in front of the pair of center defenders.

Coaching the 4-3-3

As they are in numerical equality against the rival pair of strikers, they will not be able to show too much aggression and that is why the center mid fielder's levelheaded coverage in front of the defense becomes fundamental.

On the flanks our side chain formed by the side back, inside mid fielder and wing are the natural stand-off against the opposing trio made up of the side defender, center mid fielder and side mid fielder.

In cases where the opponent is technically brilliant and it is difficult for us to contrast him in the middle of the field it is a good idea to ask the wings to make deep movements back (changing what is a 4-3-3 during the possession phase into a 4-5-1 during the phase of non-possession) so as not to force the side back to lengthen out the defense diagonal on the weak side.

4-3-3 against 4-3-3.

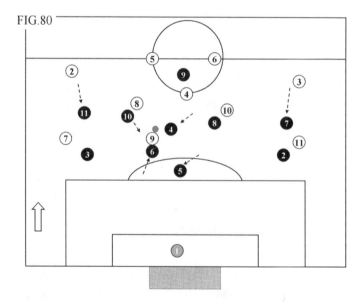

In this situation our two center defenders will be playing in numerical superiority against the opponents' center of attack.

It is important to make as much as we can of the two against one situation (one of the center defenders anticipates and shortens up tightly on the center forward while the other gives him coverage) so as to limit the play being made by the most advanced member of the opposition.

With regard to the clashes between our side defenders and the opposing wings, the best thing is not to ask our side backs to tighten up the diagonal 'inside the field' so as to improve their position against the opponents' side backs, taking away time and playing space from them even when they are not in possession. We will be expecting a more aggressive attitude from the center mid fielder so as to help his section team mates resolve their individual contrasts against the direct adversaries.

4-3-3 against 4-3-1-2.

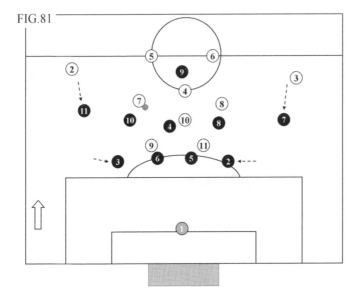

FIG.81

Coaching the 4-3-3

With our center mid fielder at work on the opponents' 3/4 line and our two center defenders playing against the two rival strikers, it will be the side defenders' task to give solidity in the center of the section by tightening up the inside diagonal.

This movement will permit the back section to look after any possible break-ins without the ball made by the opponents' finishing touch player (n. 10), and it will give protection to the center defenders.

The wings can move far back to guarantee the control along the flanks if the opponents are breaking into these parts of the field with too much ease.

Along the flanks our half-wings will need to be good at limiting their rival inside mid fielders' playing time and space. To do so they will have to move back and double up on the defenders whenever necessary.

4-3-3 against 3-4-1-2.

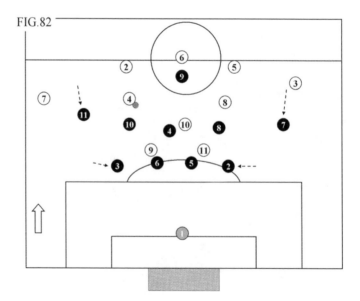

FIG.82

In the tactical face-off against the 3-4-1-2 it is necessary once again to close off the opposing triangle formed by the ☐ player in collaboration with the center strikers.

The principles to be followed are those that we have already seen in preceding sections. The only difference is relative to a useful shift made to block the opposing side players' in-depth break-ins. If we do not like the idea of bringing our wings too far back we can ask our side defender on the strong side not to tighten up the diagonal too much (which, instead, the defender on the strong side will be doing) so as to be ready to hinder the opposing side player's break-ins.

4-3-3 against 5-3-2.

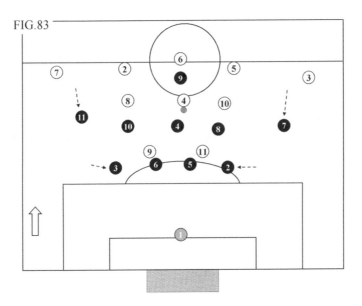

FIG.83

The section face-off in the middle of the field starts off with a situation of numerical equality (3 against 3).
To avoid the creation of numerical equality at the center of our defense, the two side backs need to tighten the diagonal towards the inside when the ball is in the central zone (cf. Fig. 83)

Coaching the 4-3-3

When the ball is along the flanks (Fig. 84), while the side back on the strong side moves towards that zone, the side back on the weak side tightens the diagonal so that the center defenders can play in numerical superiority against the opponents' three-man attack.

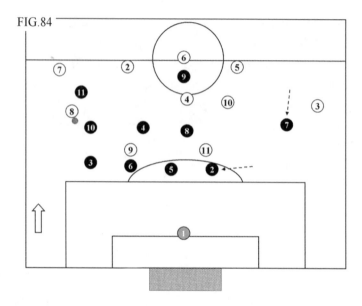

FIG.84

A long clearance will be covered by the wing moving back on the weak side.

STEP 7

GETTING THE
DEFENSE PHASE
ACROSS

The tactical organization of the defense must, in my opinion, begin with the line of the back section.

From there you will move on to the tactical formation of the mid fielders, followed by the integration (i.e., the structural organization of tasks and movements) of the defense and mid field sections.

Your work on defense organization will terminate when even the attacking players have been involved and they have achieved their own preset tactical targets in the project.

In what follows I will be giving a useful outline on how to get all this across (it has in fact already been well analyzed in the book Soccer's 4-4-2 System) so that the coach will be able to plan his work on the field.

ESSENTIAL EXERCISES IN ORGANIZING THE DEFENSE SECTION.

1. Collective movements leading to the movement of the ball.

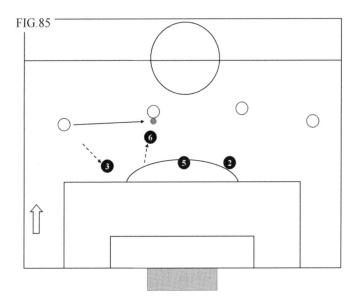

FIG.85

The four defenders are lined up on the defense half of the field and they have to move in connection with the horizontal passes carried out by the sparring opposition.

The defense section will then begin to 'draw' diagonals (on side balls) and pyramids (central balls) on the field.

2. Two against two (center and sides)

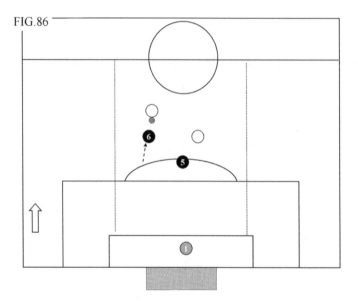

FIG.86

This is a very important exercise in training pairs of players in giving reciprocal coverage. It is carried out both in the central zone (by the pair of center defenders as shown in Fig. 86) and on the sides (by a pair made up of the center and side defenders).

This exercise gives the players the key to containing filtered balls, dump and rebound passes, cuts, combinations and overlapping. Here you have two attacking players in possession. They have to score in the goal defended by the keeper after having got past the opposition of the two defenders.

3. 4 against 6.

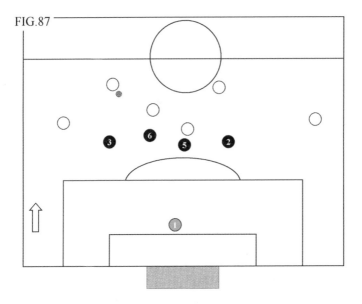

This exercise takes place in the defense half of the field with four defenders trying to carry out zonal defense mechanisms in order to stop the attacking players (in numerical superiority) from shooting at goal.

AN ESSENTIAL EXERCISE IN THE ORGANIZATION OF THE BLOCK MADE UP OF THE DEFENSE AND MID FIELD SECTIONS.

1. 7 against 9.

The defense and mid field sections play in numerical inferiority against the opponents so that the mid fielders can improve their tightening up movements (doubling up, integration, shifting) in reference to the defenders.

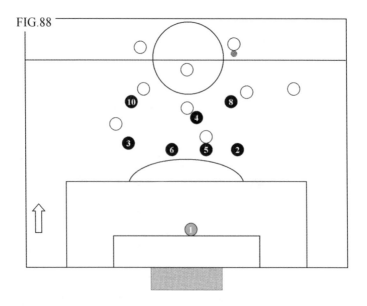

FIG.88

AN ESSENTIAL EXERCISE IN THE ORGANIZATION OF THE BLOCK MADE UP OF THE MID FIELD SECTIONS AND ATTACK.

1. 7 (+ 4) against 11.

The aim of this exercise is to improve the movements to be made in ultra offensive pressing.

In the attacking half of the field, the mid field and attacking sections (7 players) have to force the opposing team into making long clearances.

The exercise begins when the coach passes the ball to one of the backs in the training team.

When the attacking players have regained possession the exercise starts over from the beginning.

During this exercise it is important to modify the tactical set up of the sparring opposition so that the players of the 4-3-3 are forced to change their forward shifts and the movements to create pressure depending on the tactical context.

FIG.89

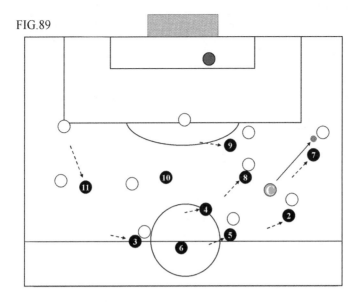

AN ESSENTIAL EXERCISE IN COLLECTIVE ORGANIZATION.

1. 11 against 0 (shadow match).

The team is lined up on the field and moves in response to the coach's indications. He gives them collective orientation (shortening up to the front or back) and selects the player who is to come out in pressure.

STEP 8

COACHING THE TRANSITION

Up to this point we have been concentrating singly on one or the other of the two principle phases of play that characterize the game of soccer - the attacking phase and the defending phase. Our aim was to give the players instruction in how to learn and grasp the various tactical principles of these individual phases.

However, if we want to give our team a first class sense of organization it is absolutely necessary to provide for specific exercises that coach the team in ways of adapting to changes in the situation.

In practice, we must make sure that our players know how to change attitude when they have recovered possession by making a speedy switch from the defense to the attacking phase (positive transition). We need also to give them instruction on the opposite situation, i.e., when the team loses possession and we need to go at once from the possession to the defense phase (negative transition).

The team will not always be able to start their attacking play with the ball in the keeper's possession or to begin defending after a shot at the opposing goal. They will not always have time and means to get back into a defense position.

When coaching transition, you must consider working in sequence on both these phases. You will be using what we call multi phase exercises.

COACHING POSITIVE TRANSITION.

In order to give complete coaching in how to change tactical attitude once you have regained possession you must include exercises which involve one main section of the team after the other.

Coaching the 4-3-3

The first exercise we will be looking at specifically concerns the defense section.

1. Block of 7 + 3 attacking players against 10 opponents.

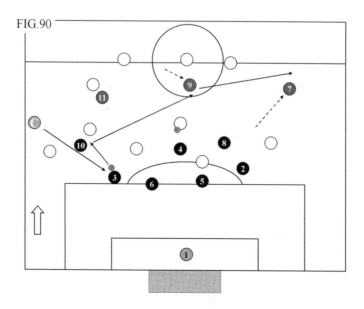

The team fielded with the 4-3-3 is defending in the defense half of the field against opponents who begin the exercise in possession and whose aim it is to shoot on goal.

As the phase of non-possession proceeds, the coach will pass his ball to one of the four backs (in the example, the left side back) so forcing the team to change mode.

When the defender has gained possession, he makes the best possible defensive outlet and his team has to bring the ball as quickly as possible over the mid field line while the opponents try to hold them back.

2. 11 against 0 with interruptions.

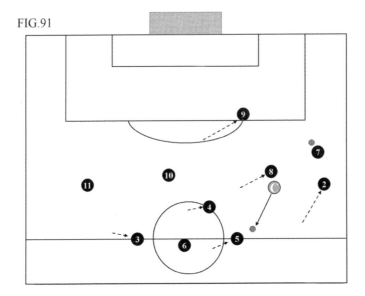

FIG.91

The team sets up attacking play in the offensive half of the field along the classic lines of 11 against 0. At a certain point the coach puts a new ball on the field, forcing the players to restart play adapting themselves to the new tactical situation. When the team has reached a good level of play, you can put a series of balls on the field in close succession, so forcing the players to make continuous adjustments.

3. 4 + 3 against 4.

This exercise is used in coaching breaks.
Position the block made up of the mid fielders and the strikers in the attacking half (or even in a position slightly further back).
A defense section of 4 or 5 players is positioned to oppose them.

FIG.92

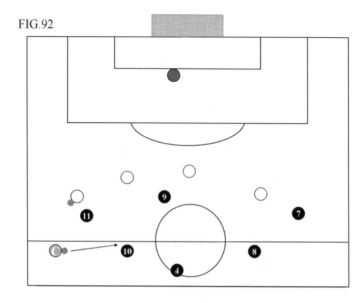

The exercise begins with the opposing defense group in possession. They are passing the ball around as they come forward, encouraged by the fact that our three strikers are only pretending to disturb their play.

At a certain point, the coach puts a new ball on the field, kicking it in the direction of one of the members of the team being coached. This will modify the tactical situation and will cause the block of 7 players to start off their play as quickly as they can so as to attack the opponents' badly positioned defense.
Each action should develop almost exclusively in vertical lines (following finishing touch principles) and must be as quick and sharp as possible.

COACHING NEGATIVE TRANSITION

Instruction on negative transition follows the same principles as those regarding positive transition.

The aim of the exercises described below is to improve and give uniformity to the team's tactical conduct in relation to the part (the depth) of the field where the opponents have regained possession.

1. 11 against 11 in the attacking half of the field.

Our team begins the exercise in possession with the aim of getting past the opponents.

At a certain point the tactical set up will be changed by the arrival of a new ball on the field (kicked by the coach towards one of the opponents).

Starting with the attacking players, our team will have to switch as quickly as possible into the defense phase so that they can regain possession before the opponents get over the 3/4 line on the field.

FIG.93

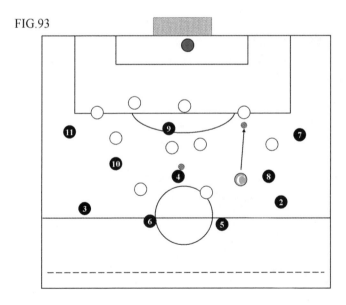

2. 11 against 11 on the whole field.

This exercise is almost exactly the same as the last. The only important differences are that the coach will give the ball to the opponents in the middle segment of the field and he will pass it most frequently to a mid fielder.

Here you are coaching negative transition mainly in the block composed of the defenders and the mid fielders.

3. 4 + 1 against 10 opponents

This exercise is used specifically to coach transition and how to manage with numerical inferiority in the block made up of the four defenders and the center mid fielder.

To begin with, however, the whole team is involved, starting off from a position in defense with the aim of opening up an attacking action.

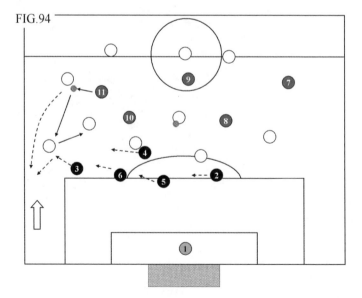

FIG.94

When the coach blows the whistle the team in possession lets the opponents have the ball. They take quick repossession and initiate a counter attack.

The players belonging to the block in question (4 + 1) will have to face their opponents' break back and they may well find themselves forced to defend in numerical inferiority.

CONCLUSIONS

My idea was to write a book that would be easy to consult and which would analyze in a suitably wide-ranging way the most important aspects which a coach will have to keep in mind when he decides to implement the 4-3-3 system.

I hope that in reading this book you have found ideas and incentives which will be useful in carrying out your work on the field.

Massimo Lucchesi
m.lucchesi@allenatore.net

BONUS EXERCISES

SHORT CENTRAL ATTACKS

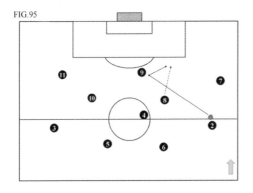

THE SIDE BACK PLAYS THE BALL TO THE CENTER FORWARD. HE MAKES A DUMP IMMEDIATELY ON THE INSIDE MIDFIELDER WHO IS BREAKING IN AND WHO WILL THEN SHOOT.

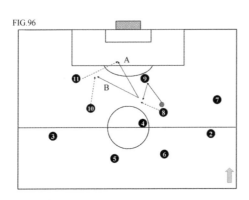

THE INSIDE MIDFIELDER IS IN POSSESSION. BY INTERACTING WITH THE CENTER FORWARD HE GIVES HIS TEAMMATES THE CHANCE TO GO INTO DEPTH.

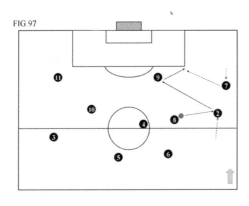

THE SIDE BACK RECEIVES THE BALL ALONG THE FLANK WHILE THE WING CREATES SPACE BY CUTTING INTO THE FIELD. THE PLAY FINISHES WITH THE CENTER MIDFIELDER'S DUMP ON THE SIDE STRIKER AS HE BREAKS INTO SPACE. HE WILL THEN SHOOT.

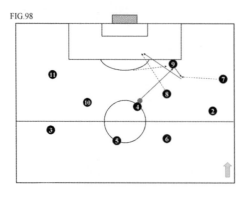

THE CENTER MID FIELDER
PASSES TO THE CENTER
FORWARD AS HE BREAKS
AWAY FROM MARKING SO
FREEING SPACE IN THE CENTER
TO BE USED BY THE INSIDE
MID FIELDER. THE CENTER
FORWARD LEAVES THE BALL
TO THE WING WHO GIVES
THE ASSIST TO THE INSIDE
MID FIELDER AS HE BREAKS IN.

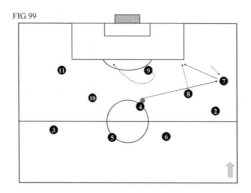

THE CENTER MID FIELDER
MAKES A CHANGE OF PLAY
FOR THE WING, WHO, BY
STAYING WIDE, CREATES
SPACE FOR THE INSIDE MID
FIELDER TO BREAK INTO
VERTICALLY. HE WILL TAKE THE
SHOT.

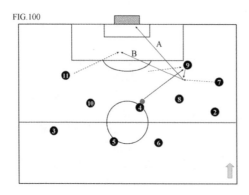

THE CENTER MID FIELDER
PASSES TO THE CENTER
FORWARD AS HE BREAKS
AWAY FROM MARKING SO
FREEING SPACE IN THE CENTER
FOR THE WING WHO
RECEIVES HIS DUMP AND CAN
EITHER SHOOT OR PASS TO
THE WING ON THE WEAK
SIDE AS HE CUTS TOWARDS
THE GOAL.

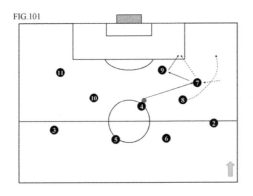

FIG.101

THE CENTER MIDFIELDER OPENS ON THE WING, WHO FREES HIMSELF FOR THE SHOT AFTER A COMBINATION WITH THE CENTER FORWARD.

SHORT SIDE ATTACKS

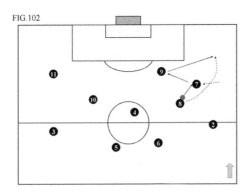

FIG.102

CHAIN COMBINATION BETWEEN THE WING, CENTER FORWARD AND INSIDE MIDFIELDER IN ORDER TO FREE THE LAST FOR THE CROSS

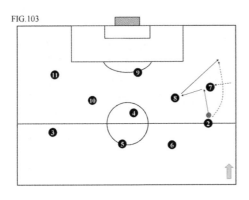

FIG.103

CHAIN COMBINATION BETWEEN THE INSIDE MIDFIELDER, WING AND SIDE DEFENDER IN ORDER TO FREE THE LAST FOR THE CROSS.

Coaching the 4-3-3

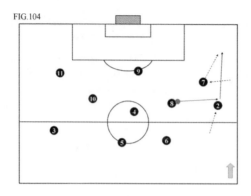

FIG.104

THE WING CUTS INTO THE FIELD FREEING SPACE FOR THE DESCENT OF THE SIDE BACK, WHO RECEIVES THE BALL FROM THE INSIDE MID FIELDER. THE SIDE BACK WILL THEN PASS TO THE WING WHO FIRST HAS FIRST MADE AN 'IN-OUT' MOVEMENT BEFORE CARRYING OUT THE CROSS.

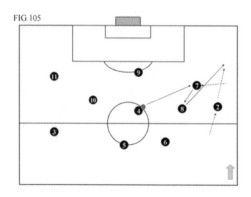

FIG.105

SIDE CHAIN COMBINATION USEFUL FOR BRING THE SIDE BACK TO THE CROSS

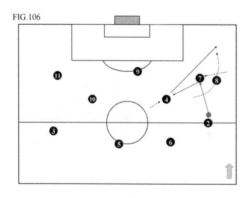

FIG.106

THE SIDE BACK PASSES VERTICALLY TO THE WING, WHO FOLLOWS BY DUMPING ON THE CENTER MID FIELDER. HE PLAYS TOWARDS THE FLANK TO THE INSIDE MID FIELDER WHO HAS OVERLAPPED AND CAN NOW CROSS.

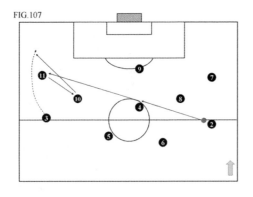

THE SIDE BACK PASSES TO THE CENTER MIDFIELDER. HE MAKES AN IMMEDIATE CHANGE OF PLAY FOR THE WING, WHO IS STAYING WIDE. YOU THEN CARRY OUT A SIDE CHAIN COMBINATION WITH THE SIDE BACK OVERLAPPING AND RECEIVING THE BALL FROM THE INSIDE MIDFIELDER.

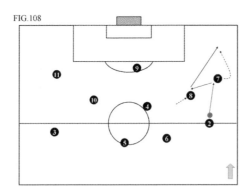

HAVING FREED HIMSELF OF MARKING, THE WING RECEIVES THE BALL FROM THE SIDE BACK. HE THEN INTERACTS WITH THE INSIDE MIDFIELDER TO FREE HIMSELF FOR THE CROSS.

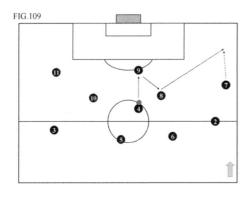

THE CENTER MIDFIELDER MAKES A VERTICAL PASS TO THE CENTER FORWARD, WHO IMMEDIATELY DUMPS ON THE INSIDE MIDFIELDER. HE OPENS OUT TO THE SIDE FOR THE WING, WHO CAN CARRY OUT THE CROSS.

LONG CENTRAL ATTACKS

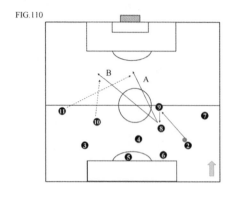

FIG.110

THE SIDE BACK PASSES VERTICALLY TO THE CENTER FORWARD, WHO DUMPS ON THE INSIDE MID FIELDER. HE THEN FILTERS THE BALL TO THE WING OR THE INSIDE MID FIELDER ON THE WEAK SIDE, WHO GET FREE OF MARKING INTO DEPTH AFTER MAKING A COMBINED MOVEMENT.

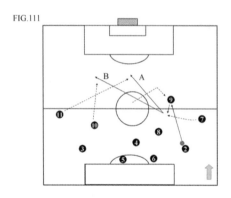

FIG.111

THE SIDE BACK PASSES VERTICALLY TO THE CENTER FORWARD, WHO FREES HIMSELF OF MARKING BY MAKING A COUNTER MOVEMENT. THE CENTER STRIKER PASSES INTERNALLY TO THE WING WHO HAS CUT INSIDE THE FIELD. THE WING PUTS ON THE FINISHING TOUCHES BY FILTERING THE BALL EITHER TOWARDS THE INSIDE MID FIELDER OR TO THE WING WHO GETS FREE OF MARKING BY CUTTING TOWARDS THE CENTER OF THE WEAK SIDE.

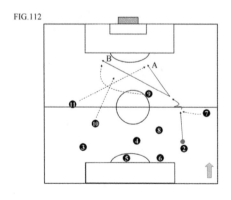

FIG.112

THE SIDE BACK CATCHES THE WING WHO FREES HIMSELF OF MARKING BY CUTTING INSIDE THE FIELD. THE WING WILL THEN FILTER THE BALL TO ONE OF HIS TEAM MATES WHO HAVE MOVED QUICKLY INTO DEPTH.

148

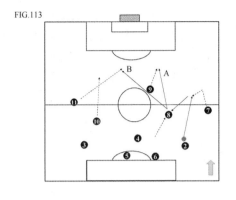

FIG.113

THE SIDE BACK PLAYS THE BALL TO THE CENTER FORWARD. HE MAKES A DUMP THE SIDE BACK CATCHES THE WING, WHO DUMPS ON THE INSIDE MID FIELDER AND MOVES AWAY. INSTEAD OF PASSING SIDEWAYS TO THE WING AS SEEN IN A PRECEDING EXAMPLE, THE INSIDE MIDFIELDER FILTERS THE BALL TO THE CENTER FORWARD, WHO HAS BROKEN FREE OF MARKING INTO DEPTH IMMEDIATELY ON THE INSIDE MIDFIELDER WHO IS BREAKING IN AND WHO WILL THEN SHOOT.

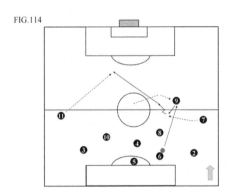

FIG.114

THE CENTER BACK PASSES LONG TO THE CENTER FORWARD. THE WING GOES TO RECEIVE HIS DUMP AND THEN FILTERS THE BALL TO THE WING ON THE OTHER SIDE.

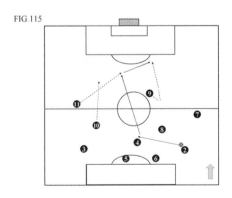

FIG.115

THE SIDE BACK OPENS IN THE MIDDLE FOR THE CENTER MIDFIELDER, WHO PASSES VERTICALLY FOR THE WING'S CUT-IN ON THE WEAK SIDE SO HE CAN RECEIVE THE BALL INSIDE THE FIELD. THE WING CARRIES OUT QUICK FINISHING TOUCHES FOR THE CENTER FORWARD WHO HAS BROKEN INTO SPACE.

FIG.116

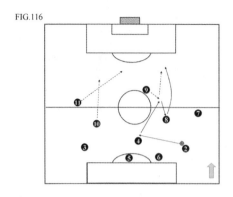

THE SIDE BACK OPENS CENTRALLY ON THE CENTER MID FIELDER. HE PASSES VERTICALLY TO THE CENTER FORWARD, WHO INTERACTS WITH THE INSIDE MID FIELDER TO RECEIVE IN DEPTH.

LONG SIDE ATTACKS

FIG.117

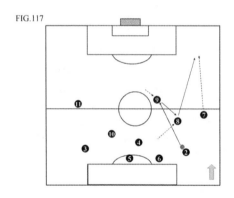

THE SIDE BACK MAKES A VERTICAL PASS FOR THE CENTER FORWARD, WHO DUMPS ON THE INSIDE MID FIELDER. HE THEN CATCHES THE WING WHO IS BREAKING IN ALONG THE FLANK.

FIG.118

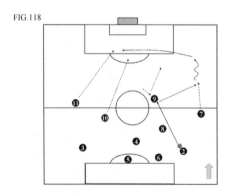

THE SIDE BACK PASSES VERTICALLY TO THE CENTER FORWARD, WHO IMMEDIATELY SENDS THE WING INTO DEPTH. HE CARRIES OUT FINISHING TOUCHES BY CROSSING FOR THE OTHER WING OR THE INSIDE MID FIELDER BREAKING INTO SPACE ALONG THE WEAK SIDE.

FIG.119

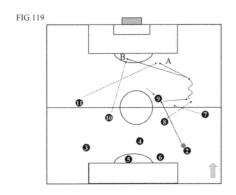

THE SIDE BACK PASSES VERTICALLY TO THE CENTER FORWARD WHILE THE INSIDE MIDFIELDER AND THE WING CROSS OVER SO AS TO KNOCK THE ZONAL DEFENSE ORGANIZATION OFF BALANCE. THE CENTER FORWARD DUMPS ON THE INSIDE MIDFIELDER WHO HAS BROKEN OUT TOWARDS THE FLANK AND HE WILL THEN CARRY OUT FINISHING TOUCHES.

FIG.120

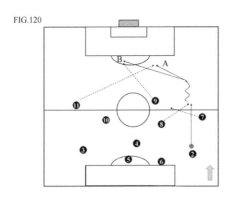

THE SIDE BACK PASSES ALONG THE FLANK TO THE INSIDE MIDFIELDER AFTER HE HAS CROSSED OVER WITH THE WING. THE MIDFIELDER IN POSSESSION WILL THEN FILTER THE BALL TO ONE OF HIS TEAMMATES WHO IS BREAKING IN.

FIG.121

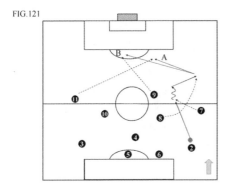

THE SIDE BACK CATCHES THE WING, WHO HAS COME TO RECEIVE THE BALL IN THE CENTER. HE WILL THEN PASS TO THE INSIDE MIDFIELDER WHO HAS CROSSED OVER AND FREED HIMSELF ON THE FLANK. THE MIDFIELDER THEN CARRIES OUT FINISHING TOUCHES FOR ONE OF HIS TEAMMATES CUTTING INTO DEPTH.

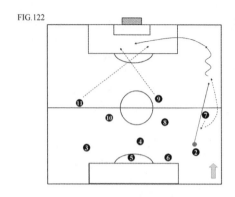

FIG.122

THE SIDE BACK PASSES LONG AND CATCHES THE WING WHO HAS BROKEN FREE OF MARKING AFTER HAVING MADE A LONG-SHORT MOVEMENT. THE SIDE STRIKER WILL THEN CARRY OUT FINISHING TOUCHES BY CROSSING TO HIS TEAM MATES IN THE AREA.

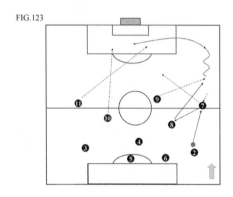

FIG.123

THE INSIDE MID FIELDER IS IN THE SIDE BACK PASSES VERTICALLY TO THE WING, WHO DUMPS ON THE INSIDE MID FIELDER. HE PASSES TO THE CENTER FORWARD WHO HAS FREED HIMSELF ON THE FLANK AND CAN THEN MAKE THE CROSS.POSSESSION. BY INTERACTING WITH THE CENTER FORWARD HE GIVES HIS TEAM MATES THE CHANCE TO GO INTO DEPTH.

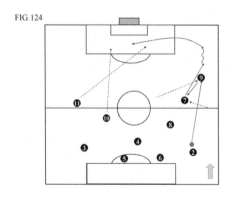

FIG.124

THE SIDE BACK PLAYS VERTICALLY TO THE CENTER FORWARD WHO HAS FREED HIMSELF ON THE FLANKS. ONCE HE HAS RECEIVED THE BALL, HE DUMPS ON THE WING FOR A COMBINATION THAT WILL THEN ALLOW HIM TO CROSS.

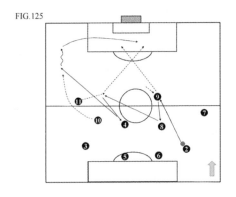

FIG.125

THE SIDE BACK PASSES LONG AND CATCHES THE WING WHO HAS BROKEN FREE OF MARKING AFTER HAVING THIS PLAY STARTS OFF WITH A VERTICAL PASS FOR THE STRIKER, WHO DUMPS ON THE SUPPORTING INSIDE MIDFIELDER. HE THEN CHANGES PLAY FOR THE WING AS HE CUTS INTO THE FIELD OPENING UP SPACE FOR THE INSIDE MIDFIELDER TO BREAK INTO. THE INSIDE MIDFIELDER CROSSES AFTER RECEIVING THE PASS FROM THE CENTER MIDFIELDER MADE A LONG-SHORT MOVEMENT. THE SIDE STRIKER WILL THEN CARRY OUT FINISHING TOUCHES BY CROSSING TO HIS TEAMMATES IN THE AREA.